MW00899413

"You have to wonder at times what you're doing out there. Over the years, I've given myself a thousand reasons to keep running, but it always comes back to where it started. It comes down to self-satisfaction and a sense of achievement." -Steve Prefontaine

For my mom Ellen Zinner (1943-2015). Thanks for giving us all that you had. Your love, kindness, and strength live on.

Chapter 1

"If it weren't for running, I may have put a bullet in the back of my head years ago."

"Surely you exaggerate."

"Perhaps." Denny and Keith both let the spoken words drift aimlessly into the atmosphere, abundant with snowflakes which continued to delicately fall from the milky grey, winter sky. Their running shoes made a gentle, rhythmic sound when they momentarily made contact with the snow-covered surface. The D&L Trail stretched ahead, then started to bend around a sweeping turn which loosely paralleled the course the Lehigh River took as it wound through the valley, until all of it just sort of dissolved into a fuzzy whiteness. It was, in a word, perfect.

Denny heard the low-pitched rumble of a train, slowly chugging its way southbound somewhere along the opposite side of the frigid, flowing waters of the river. The train blew its horn twice, as it likely approached a street crossing. Denny scanned with slightly squinted eyes across and up the other side of the river, but he could not catch any discernable sight of a freight train. But he listened rather intently as the sound became gradually quieter and quieter; Denny strained to hear even the slightest trace of echoes coming through the bare, stripped trees lining either side of the

Lehigh, until he could hear nothing more, and the train was gone for good.

"Gosh I'm hungry." The sound of Keith's voice startled Denny, who for the past few minutes had forgotten that he even had company running alongside him. "I hope Suzanne is cooking up something for dinner," he added with a slight laugh, as the two runners continued their easy pace along the wide trail, part of a hundred plus mile rails to trails project started several years after Denny had moved away. It took its name, or acronym, from the Delaware and Lehigh River corridors. Save for a few disconnected sections, one could get all the way into Philadelphia following its route. Today though, they had another mile and a half or so to run in the other direction to return to the trailhead by Dunbar's beer distributor, a large warehouse near where Keith had parked his car.

Denny got back up to the converted house apartment after the short drive, took off his Garmin watch and set it down on a small table by the door and took a long look about the place. A mattress, with a heavy blanket, comforter, and a pillow sort of haphazardly strewn on top, laid in the middle of the bare wooden floor. There was a small table on top of which was a boom box stereo, like something out of the 1980s, with a twenty-ounce water bottle and big coffee mug setting beside it. Clothes appeared to bubble out of a dark green duffel bag laying on the floor near the far wall, and beneath a solitary window with half opened plastic blinds dangling in front of. A pile of some books, a notebook and a training log, were neatly stacked up against the wall.

"Hmmph," Denny said aloud as he walked over into an empty second room and began taking off his cold, damp clothes and slowly, systematically hanging them over an open lawn chair he had placed near the oil heater; one of those radiators he could recall seeing in his grandparent's house. A bare, exposed light bulb hung from the ceiling in a tight hallway that connected the two rooms to a half-furnished kitchen at the other end of the apartment. Denny wasted little more time getting into the creaky old tub in the closet like bathroom and took as warm of a shower as he could.

The snow outside continued to steadily fall, covering by now the road and the side-walks with two to three inches of fluffy white powder. Down the street a couple of kids carried on throwing snow balls back and forth, as they would dart and duck behind parked cars to avoid being pelted by each other. They all came to a halt for a few seconds as a car slowly drove down the street. The car's headlights illuminated one of the younger boys, who couldn't have been much older than ten, as he stood there and waited to resume playing. His winter jacket and beanie were speckled in white from all the snow sticking to it. Denny watched in silence from out the side window on the second floor; a few moments later they were all gone from his view, off no doubt to further winter time adventures. A peculiar sadness lightly washed over Denny, as he turned away from the window and sat down on the mattress. Perhaps Thomas Wolfe was correct; you can't go home again.

The following morning some light snow had begun to fall again, as Denny walked down the narrow, slippery stair case which served as the entrance way to the apartment and was located on the one side of the old, two-story house. The stairs themselves led onto the sidewalks of South Second Street. A north to westerly wind was blowing, which laced the air with a shivery bite, as Denny assiduously tucked the long sleeves of his outer heavier shirt into his gloves before hitting start on his watch. He slowly and somewhat guardedly began to run downhill on the sidewalk, but after almost slipping, he decided it would be advantageous to run on the road itself, which seemed to have better footing, especially inside of the tracks vehicles had made in the snow. It was still quite early on a Saturday so there shouldn't be much traffic out anyway Denny reasoned, as he clapped his hands together twice to generate a little body heat. But he knew from experience he would warm up in due time during the run.

And once he began to settle into the run, Denny remembered how much he used to love running in the snow. It was at times like being inside one's own snow globe; such impressions intensified once he had exited the town and had begun climbing into the heights of Mahoning Township. Everything was coated in white; all the tree branches, shrubs, fences, power lines, roof tops, as the snow continued to drop down from out of the clouds, which themselves seemed to be suspended no more than a couple hundred feet above the ground. The whole sky looked like a giant sagging marshmallow squeezing out miniature cotton balls that harmlessly fell onto whatever lie beneath. Denny felt like he was slowly climbing up into the clouds and into the snow globe itself as he crested the long, steep hill off the northwest corner of the town.

As Denny ran the ridgeline on an undulating country road, his thoughts began to drift back to days long since passed. Frequently of late he would get these vivid snapshots of a place or person from seemingly random, disjointed times in life, stretching all the way back into the more formative years of childhood. Some of these reminisces came charged with sensations powerful enough to sort of flood Denny; it would all feel so tangible and overwhelmingly real, these haphazard, helter-skelter luminous flashes, before they'd inevitably fade away, and on back into the cavernous recesses of the past. Denny liked to chase these ephemeral memories and follow their tracks, like a hunter stalking its prey. Often times he'd abruptly encounter a dead end; the trail would vanish into thin air. Or he'd stumble upon something tangentially related, and diligently pursue such quarry.

Denny pondered that perhaps he was becoming some kind of holistic visionary, bestowed with magical powers to see beyond the normal façade of reality. Was he becoming unfettered from the physics of time and space? And did these snapshots, these memories contain clues hidden deep within their riddles? And if so, what were they clues to? Or perhaps in a more truthful light, he was simply having some sort of slowly developing nervous breakdown, perpetuated by an apparent unquenchable thirst to push beyond the parameters of the very finite five senses human beings are born with. Either way, Denny felt like it was his vision quest to take, and he was far too curious not to see where all of this seemingly nonsensical stuff just might lead. And it had all lead him today to this snow-covered road outside of the small town he had been born and raised in; and it was here that he ran.

Just then Denny found himself approaching a cluster of houses, one of which Traci Jean used to live in. After all these years he recognized the house from afar, with its long extended front porch, the sloping backyard with an in-ground pool and redwood deck. His mood became somber, reverent as he made his way past the gravel driveway and front yard. Denny said a prayer and added aloud, "God rest your soul Traci Jean." It had to have been almost three years since she had passed, maybe four? And it seemed so sad and strange to be remembering and honoring an old track and cross-country teammate in such a solemn way. A couple of years back he had written her name on a pair of running shoes he wore while turning dozens of laps at the annual Relay for Life in Wilmington, North Carolina; the last he had heard from her, she was actively involved with the fund-raising event up here. Somewhere packed away in an old shoe box he still had a photo of the two of them taken at senior prom.

A little farther down the road, past the house where he had spent many a memorable night of his halcyon youth, the landscape opened up, affording Denny a view into the valley; a view partially shrouded by the wintry weather that continued to lightly, yet methodically persist. He ran past an old farmhouse just off to one of the sides of the road, and for several precious moments the only things audible were the somewhat muted sound of his running shoes hitting the snow-covered road, and the muffled din being created by thousands of snowflakes landing on the trees and fields, which swept back down the rolling hills to his left, and on back up the small mountain to his right. This must be what heaven is like, Denny thought as he ran on, and began the precipitous descent downward into the floor of the valley.

Back on South Second Street, and in front again of the house in which Keith had spent the better part of a year converting into four apartments, Denny looked at his watch which read 12.62 miles, in an elapsed time of 1:44:38. Not too shabby he thought. And he also thought that maybe he'd get a few more miles in later in the evening, though Denny was trying to avoid two-a-days after reading *Running with the Buffaloes*, and about how fitness gains are maximized more through only running "singles." But he was getting a kick out of running many of the roads he had cut his teeth on as a scholastic runner twenty plus years ago. And the hills were such an invigorating challenge; he hadn't realized how much he had missed such terrain, and just how hilly it was back up here. Much different form where he now lived right at the coast, running for the most part in the "flatlands", as it was referred to in the sport's circles.

Denny grabbed ahold of the metal rail and slowly walked up the steps; he told himself that he would decide later, and maybe see if Keith wanted to run with him again. The snow had stopped falling, and the sun seemed determined to break through the cloud cover. Its hazy outline was barely visible part way up the eastern sky, though Denny wished it would just continue to snow and snow.

Perhaps the weather served to obscure his perception of reality just slightly enough; stilting any foreboding thoughts surely present just below the surface conscience.

Later, as Denny sat on his lawn chair and ate a big bowl of homemade ham and bean soup that Suzanne had sent over, such aforementioned thoughts seemed to break through, just as the sun had by now pierced through the afternoon sky. The snow too had mostly melted or been blown off the big oak trees in the adjacent backyards within Denny's view, revealing the drabber browns and greys, that are such a ubiquitous part of wintertime's palette, particularly in the north. He watched the trees sway back and forth, as he slowly brought one spoonful after the next of the delicious soup to his mouth, savoring the flavors on his tongue, and the warmth of the soup as it slid down his throat and into his belly. This buoyed his spirits some, though Denny knew he could be one petulant, moody son of a bitch.

He did decide to go for a second run, after darkness had cloaked the town. Denny bundled up almost every inch of his six-foot lithe frame, but at the last moment decided to wear shorts instead of track pants, as he had the urge to air it out and run a few, faster miles. The night itself seemed to welcome him; Denny felt more comfortable under the cover of darkness, like a thief that no one could quite get a visual fix on. He could stay hidden in the shadows, able to absorb whatever the town had to offer, while remaining detached, not only physically, but mentally and spiritually as well. For he had left this small, old blue-collar town for good a long time ago; fulfilling what many a young person's coming of age main ambition was, which was to get the hell out of the place. Most of the emotional connections had imperceptibly fallen away, like grains of sand falling through an hour glass, and except for his

Mom's funeral, and the occasional friend's weddings, he had barely set foot in Lehighton the past fifteen years.

Denny plotted a route which would pretty much loop the perimeter of the town; somewhere between a three to four-mile run. From the start he ran at a quicker pace, as the run took him up a small hill on South Second Street, then back down a fairly steep hill for two blocks, until he got to the flashing traffic light above the intersection of Second and Iron Streets, where he took a right and headed down another hill towards the river, before turning left by the old 7-11 convenience store and onto First Street, the main commercial district, and the street he'd follow along the eastern edge of town. A half mile or so later he passed the community park, that still had its iconic water fountain in the center. Denny remembered when he was a very young kid coming to the park in the summer for some sort of orchestral concerts performed probably by a local band, and that their older neighbors from up the street Paul and Marge Repetsky would always be there. They must be long dead now Denny surmised, as he swiftly made his way past the faintly lit, deserted park.

Further up First Street, Denny ran by a two-story building with big framed windows on either side of a wooden door, all of which was covered by a metal awning that jut out from between where the first and second floors would be. It was some sort of medical office, or business that he could recall going to as a boy with his Dad to get his glasses fixed one night. A cryptic, supernatural wave made Denny's spine sort of tingle; the whole thing kind of flashed white-hot inside of him for several seconds and seemed to claw at something deep inside a crevice in his soul. He picked up the pace even more, without realizing it; just then his watch beeped at one mile elapsed. 6:32 it read; man I'm flying, Denny whispered to himself, on top of tired legs too.

But then he turned onto Ochre Street and commenced the several blocks climb up a monstrous hill through the north side of the town. Once he had stood at the bottom of the hill during daylight and took a picture; Denny sent it to several of his running friends in North Carolina with some sort of caption like "these are the hills I grew up running on." Yes, on hills like this, which through the years of running, Denny had learned how to parcel out his efforts to successfully ascend, and to use mental tricks like breaking them up into sections, such as street to street, or even smaller divisions, such as street to alley to street. And the hills had calloused him; he would wear the badges they planted on him with pride, that sort of pride earned through hard work, run after run after run.

Once he got to Fourth, and then Fifth Street, the climb became a bit less arduous as the degree of incline dramatically decreased, before leveling off at Sixth Street, which dead ended at the base of one of the town's cemeteries. Dr. Ahner and his wife lived in a big house at the end of the street, and it amused Denny just then to imagine what they would think if they saw him out there running. It had to be pushing two decades since he had seen either of them; he had to smile inwardly at the gay times he had at all their lavish parties. They were almost Gatsby-like, at least for this place.

Denny bounded down the hill on Sixth Street as most of the feeling had returned to his legs, then rounded the corner onto Coal Street, by the baseball field with the real short right field dimensions, and headed all the way past Tenth Street, where he ran down another hill, and looped around the hospital complex where his aunt had worked night shift for most of her adult life. Occasional cars drove by on the streets, and Denny would catch the sound of some barking dogs hidden somewhere in the confines of the night, as he almost effortlessly glided past house after house. Some were lit up more than others, and as he ran by certain homes, that unmistakable flickering bluish tinted light emanating from televisions, would be cast out of windows.

And he thought about the Jack Kerouac novel *Dharma Bums*, and the description about the Japhy Ryders of the world out prowling around in the wilderness, while most of the rest of civilization was safely ensconced indoors. Denny could feel a kinship with such mad characters; there was a bit of ecstasy in his gait, and in the wispy little puffs of air that danced out of his mouth when he exhaled. In fact, he suddenly felt like laughing out loud at all of it all.

Back home, and back inside the apartment, Denny turned on the boom box stereo to Z95, his favorite radio station while growing up. A Led Zeppelin song "The Rover" came on, and at one point he even jumped up onto the mattress and began to play a little air guitar, as he thought about Trent, and how he ought to look him up soon. Maybe he'd want to go for a run.

A few days later he met Trent in the front parking lot of their old high school. Dusk was slowly beginning to overtake the winter sky; as the sunlight began to diminish, the air bore more of a frosty chill. They had about thirty minutes tops of daylight left until the sun dropped for good behind the rolling hills to the west, as the two former teammates headed out to run the six-mile BZ Farms course. Which was a run they had set forth on and completed innumerable times; the name was derived from the Christmas tree farm located at about the half way point. Denny noticed that Trent seemed to be carrying a little extra weight on his five-foot eight-inch frame, but then again, he was built a little more like a football player, or the wrestler he used to be. That being said, he always had such a great running engine or aerobic capacity; he could seemingly get into pretty good running shape at the drop of a hat. Though they certainly weren't kids anymore, like when their paths first crossed back in the third grade, as members of the same Booster Club Track and Field team.

Trent was pushing the tempo rather frisky from the get go, which Denny made immediate note of. "Dang. You getting out here a lot?" he asked.

"No. Mostly the treadmill. Winter weather always sucks. Dark too early too," Trent answered between breaths. When they got about two miles outside of the town to the west, the pace slowed considerably as the two runners began climbing a moderate hill, which then crested, and dipped downward while bending around a wide curve which led to the intersection of the road that passed through BZ Farms. As they ran on, Trent asked, "how long are you up here for?"

"I have no idea," Denny succinctly replied.

By the time they wound their way through the cluster of homes adjacent to the dozens of acres of pine trees, it was about dark. Denny noticed the moon now visible and about three quarters full, as it appeared to be comfortably resting on top of the Mahoning Mountain, which lurked just off in the direction they were headed. Dim, barely perceptible shadows were cast onto the road from the occasional bare trees that dotted the barren fields on either side of the road. The nighttime air was perfectly still, and everything around them seemed so unequivocally silent. Denny felt as if he had to say something more; being beckoned not only by the curiosity of his good friend, but by the optics and acoustics of the environs.

"Couple of weeks, maybe longer. Though I haven't really planned any of it out. Felt some kind of primitive urge to come back. Kind of chase things up here that I can't really define, since it's all sort of fuzzy to me. Or still in the early stages of developing."

"I see," Trent said.

"Something's been killing my spirit little by little. Maybe I just needed some time and space to think. And run a lot. Run and think. Or run and not think. I can work from home, or anywhere really, so that's cool." Denny suddenly felt the absurdity in attempting to articulate any of it, which began to amuse him on some deeper level, like black comedy.

"Little by Little. Very underrated Robert Plant song," Trent replied, though he probably understood more than Denny could have hoped for, which was quite welcome in its genuine simplicity, and empathy.

"I was jamming out to Zeppelin the other night in Keith's house. The one he fixed up. He's letting me stay there in one of the empty apartments for free."

"Nice."

They crossed the bridge which went over the Mahoning Creek. Denny looked down at the wide, rapidly flowing stream that looked so icy cold. Little splotches of snow covered parts of the scattered rocks that stuck up out of the water, as well as on some of the bare branches that hung out over the water from the edges of the woods. Denny recalled that Trent liked to fish this creek a lot; he probably still does Denny thought, but he didn't ask. Both of them climbed up out of the shallow hollow and then took a left turn onto route 443, which was lit up some from the lights of the Walmart parking lot part way up the hill, on the other side of the busier street. Trent and Denny ducked onto a dark, secondary road that cut back to Ninth Street, and then ran back on up to where they had started. The next day Trent texted Denny how later that night he had thought it was kind of cool they had met in about the exact very spot where the cross-country team used to gather at before practices and ensuing runs.

Time has a funny way of folding itself over; little occurrences from far back in the past, for a few precious, fleeting moments will suddenly feel as if they were as real as when they actually took place, or as if the interval of time between has been entirely erased. Like the way animals such as dogs have no perception of elapsed time, and everything appears and feels as if it just happened. It was all so peculiarly intriguing to Denny, and he got the intangible sense that there was some sort of unfinished business for him up here after all.

There was a particular time while Denny was in college at Penn State University, that he felt like running was the only thing keeping him together. He had started back up in earnest after taking a PE class in running the previous summer, which had also served to introduce him to a network of trails that looped in and around a golf course just off the campus. For reasons not entirely clear, a prolonged period of sadness and depression had descended over him. Denny was unmotivated scholastically, not as interested in friends or girls or parties; everything seemed perpetually grey and gloomy like the sky most days in central Pennsylvania, as that autumn slipped into winter. However, the one thing that would bring him some measure of joy, something to look forward to, and to also take a modicum of ownership and pride in, was the sport of running.

With enthusiastic verve, and bounce in his step, he invented a myriad of courses, some short, others long, some that snaked through the large sprawling campus, others that meandered onto country roads weaving through corn fields and cow pastures outside the college town. Denny wore a ten-dollar wrist watch that had a built in, very basic stopwatch; he carefully kept track of all his times with pen and paper. Records were set, and broken; he ran hard and ran often, and also ran alone. But he never once felt alone when on those roads and trails. At some point his morose mood lifted, and also that which was wont to happen to many a runner, the runs became a bit less frequent, until once again Denny was no longer an active runner.

He hadn't thought about all that in a very long time. Denny would call his Mom back then during such times, ostensibly just to chat; though sometimes he would scratch the surface as to what was negatively transpiring within. She would mainly just listen, not being the type to often proffer any concrete advice, but he always felt much better afterwards. Still, he would head out the door afterwards, to purchase any kind of cheap alcohol he could get his hands on; the kind of foul tasting crap drank only for its affects, whereby Denny would proceed to try and forget about much of anything, at least for an hour or two. He could always rationalize that the other alternatives were much more harrower and bleak. Usually music could help staunch it all temporarily too, or perhaps a good book. There were many ways he discovered to pretend and escape; years later the lines would become much too blurry.

Denny walked over and picked up a notebook from the floor and sat down on the edge of the mattress. He opened it up to a fresh page, jotted the date down in small print on the top left side above the first horizontal line. Then he wrote "I run for all the misfits out there. Those who feel an invisible tug on their souls. For those who insatiably crave something which seems to just barely allude them. But if they run a little longer, a little further, that something may just be found after all." Denny looked at it for a moment, then closed the notebook and tossed it back on the floor over by the far wall. He picked his coffee mug back up, quite warm still to the touch, and watched the steam wafting off of the surface, before dissipating into oblivion. Denny just sat there, watching; he said a little prayer for his Mom. Sometimes he wished he could still pick up that phone and dial.

Winter rolled on, as Denny flipped the page of the Philadelphia Eagles wall calendar Trent had given him to the month of February. Denny's runs rolled on too; some got a bit quicker and a bit longer, as his overall mileage started to roll on upward. The roads welcomed him daily with unconditional love; they didn't expect anything from him, make demands, or pass any kind of judgments. No, they were just there; unobtrusive, nonplussed by whatever Denny might bring forth. Both seemed quite comfortable with the parameters of the relationship.

Denny had been reading the legendry American long-distance coach Jack Daniels and was eager to delve into one of the training plans laid out in his *Daniel's Running Formula* book. He had also been diligent with what he referred to as ancillary work; mainly simple strength and core exercises like pushup and planks. Plus, all sorts of leg swings that targeted the hips and hamstrings, and exercises like lunges and squats that worked the glutes and quads. Denny would do such exercises when he took breaks from his job which he performed on his laptop, or at night while pumping out tunes on the boom box. Keith let him use free weights that were in an upstairs room above the garage, situated out behind their house, three houses down the street. All of this was being done to support the quantity of running that Denny had in mind doing. He would make notes on the sides of his running log book, keeping track of sets and numbers completed. One-night Denny joked to Trent that he felt like he was in jail, since isn't this what a lot of prisoners end up doing?

Saturday morning, he met Keith at the trailhead of the towpath; they headed northward on the wide dirt and gravel pathway, which was used in the nineteenth century by horses and mules to pull barges up and down the adjacent canal. The two fell into an easy pace, as Keith admitted he hadn't run in over a week and wasn't sure how far he'd able to go. He was about the same height as Denny but had much more of a thicker frame and muscular build. And like many people in the middle stages of life, was prone to adding a few pounds when not regularly active. Years ago, when they used to run a lot together, and enter some road races, Denny would tell him that he thought he would make a good marathon or ultra-runner, because of his natural upper body strength.

"God I'd love to be able to train more like this," Keith said about twenty minutes into the run. "Just seems like. Time constraints. Too many. Kids...always something. Long hours at work too." He was definitely feeling the effects of the run some but was grooved into it. After running a little more, Keith added, "Gotta do it or they'll find someone else. 6 months....accckkk. Company might not be there. Sucks. All over it seems to be happening."

The sun's morning rays angled through the wooded hills abutting the far side of the canal. The light thrown down helped shake off some of the cold morning air, though for February in Pennsylvania it was quite pleasant out, such as it had been the past week or two. The canal was mostly frozen over, except for a few shallower sections more exposed and out in the open. The slow, leisurely flowing waters of the Lehigh River, maybe twenty or thirty yards to their west, looked very cold still, despite the light and relative warmth of the sun being cast down upon its surface.

Denny wondered how much of the pristine, ever changing landscape Keith's eyes were seeing this morning. He felt like he should have something to say, something helpful, or encouraging, anything to his friend. But Denny doubted how much his own experiences with work and career of late would offer in any positive regards. For after a protracted period of at best enduring, and at worst being in the pit of abject misery, he one day had had enough and walked out of a large corporate environment, albeit after giving proper notice. Denny made much less money now, but the anger and helplessness continued to be drained out of him. We all make tradeoffs at times and must bear our own crosses, though if he had kids-

"I admire what you're doing out here," Keith said, after suggesting they turn around and head back. "Looking for some kind of pure way of living. Or whatever it is you are doing," he added with a laugh.

"Hell if I know. But thanks." Truth was Denny still didn't really know what exactly he was doing or why he was up there. But his instincts told him to keep running, and to keep searching, and that sometimes in order to move forward in the grander sense, one ought to double back around, and collect what perhaps was missed the first time by. He didn't know, and it didn't necessarily trouble him not to know. Denny was rather enjoying the queer state of freedom coming out of all this kind of slapdash shucking off of life's normal constraints, and doing the unexpected, which most people only get so far as to sort of wildly contemplate, when as a manner of speaking, their chips appear to be down. Sure, it wasn't always easy; Denny could be beset with doubt, plagued with waves of it at times, but he was learning to swim through it and hold fast to an internal life raft within, and enjoy the sublime moments beget from this devil-may-care undertaking.

"What does any of this matter anyway?" he added to Keith about a mile later.

"Sounds a little too existential for me bud."

Chapter 2

Denny took advantage of the warmer weather and absence of snowpack to run some of his favorite trails. Preacher's Camp was located about half way out Beltzville Lake, several miles to the east of the breast of the dam, which was built in the 1970s to create a watershed out of the Pohopoco Creek. At its head, the lake was over a half mile wide, and stretched out from the west to the east for over eight miles. There was a popular beach and swimming area, as well as a larger boat launch on the main property of the surrounding state park next to the dam, but Denny preferred the more remote access of Preacher's Camp, located at the bottom of an old, windy farm road that dropped sharply down into a small valley, and led to a parking lot where Denny parked, and changed into one of his pairs of running shoes.

He currently had five pairs with, three of which were in the back-hatch area of his Rav4. He liked to open the back up and sit in there off the end, before and after runs; it was like his own private little running office, chalk full of hundreds of multi colored flags, and several rolls of colored tape, used to mark routes utilized for workouts during cross country practices, or to mark off the courses for races held in the Carolina Beach State Park that his

USATF club put on twice a year. Denny also kept extra socks, a shirt or two, a heavier sweatshirt, and a towel in there; he never knew when something of the sort would be needed. Some trash was strewn about too, mostly in a brown crate set up against the backside of the back seats; he wasn't always the neatest person around.

Denny picked up the trailhead just to the right of the empty boat launch; after a short span the trail narrowed into a thin, single track that plunged into the thick forest, which sloped rather steep in sections back up and away from the lake's shoreline. There were a lot of tall, full bodied pine trees. The atmosphere hence was fairly dark and damp, with hints of a sweet, sappy fragrance. The surface of the trail was a mix of dirt and pine straw, with an abundance of roots and rocks that needed to be almost continually navigated. Bisecting the trail, he was running on, were several shorter trails that led from small pull offs on the farm road, down to the water's edge; fisherman would use these, and had blazed them over the course of many, many years.

One of whom was Denny's grandfather, who used to take him out here to fish when he was growing up. They would fish the lake for bass, or pike by casting their lines as far out as they could, keeping a watchful eye on the red and white plastic bobbers, while placing their rods on the ground by using twigs shaped like the letter 'Y'. They would munch on snacks, or lunch packed with affectionate care by Denny's grandmother. His grandpa would smoke his beloved Phillie cigars; "they keep the bugs away," he would say with a smile and a wink. It all seemed so familiar to Denny as he carefully snaked his way through the old growth woods.

As he got further out, the trail became even more of a challenge to run, as it would dip precipitously, then just as abruptly climb, as it devilishly wound around trees; Denny would actually grab ahold of some of the trunks with one hand to kind of steady himself as he ran horizontally across such angled inclines, while constantly watching his footing, as he would be forced to take several short, quick steps in many spots. A sort of stuttered tip toe dance; reminding him of Caballo Blanco, the eccentric, wayward hero of the novel *Born to Run*. And he thought of Caballo's trail running mantra of light, easy, free, or something like that. The almost Zen-like focus, the magic of being completely immersed in the task at hand. The hundreds of little puzzles that presented themselves; where to take the next step, and the next, and the next, which all had a way of being solved by simply doing, and not really thinking about.

There was always something primal about running in the woods, cut off from the machinations of civilization at large. Denny felt a harmonious connection with the environment, as if he was a small, yet requisite fragment of the current ecosystem he found himself in. His actions could and did spur reactions, like a squirrel scurrying up a tree, a deer warily watching his every move, the squawking of crows high up in the tree tops. Or he would have to make adjustments, such as detouring around a section of washed out trail caused by a sudden rainstorm or coming close to an animal which could potentially harm him, like a bear or a snake in defense of its territory or offspring. Out in the wilderness he was much more linked to his immediate domain, than he was when running on the open roads.

Denny followed the trail all the way to its termination point, where by then Beltzville Lake had morphed back into the Pohopoco Creek again. He glanced at his watch; just over an hour of elapsed run time, which numerically provided the symmetric challenge of completing the return journey back to Preacher's Camp in less than an hour.

That evening Denny sat on the lawn chair and ate from a bowl filled with brown rice and red beans, with jalapeno peppers and red onion cut up and mixed in. The food warmed his mouth and insides; he had let it slow cook in a big pot on the stove for a couple of hours. For the moment he was content with the monastic simplicity of his surroundings, and how it served to help him continue to appreciate on a daily basis all that he had, instead of dwelling on that which he didn't, or felt was possibly his due.

Of late Denny had become piqued with the concept of minimalism, and its growing popularity in certain strands of American culture. The concept of value, and the utilization of what one considered to be essential, and the subsequent unburdening of that which was not. The application of this philosophy to not only one's physical reality, but perhaps, and even more importantly, to our inner or spiritual life. Before Denny had packed up and headed northward, he had gone through his closet and filled up two garbage bags with articles of clothing he didn't wear much, if at all. This included probably about two dozen race shirts; Denny joked with some running friends to be on the lookout for homeless people wandering the streets while sporting such garments. Though he knew there was a time in his life when he was but a small step or two away from joining such a band of marginalized folks himself.

Denny finished his dinner and watched as darkness clothed the back yards and alleyways visible from his roost. The scattered outdoor lights attached to some of the garages and porches collectively cast a dull pale glow of light in some places, while other spaces became shrouded in the blackness of the night. Occasionally he would hear the sound of a vehicle driving on the street out front, or the bark of a lone dog somewhere not too far off. A couple kids passed on down through the alley on bikes. Winter nights in the north, despite the lack of snow cover, were such studies in quietude, so much so that Denny decided to go for a rambling walk through town. He donned a heavy sweatshirt, beanie, and a pair of gloves, and sashayed out into the inviting arms of the undiluted night.

A few days later Denny met Suzanne at six a.m. in the gravel parking lot by the D&L trailhead. It was still dark as they set off southward on the first part of the trail, which was paved with macadam as it swept its way in the shallows near the river, just below the edge of town.

"Sorry you had to get up so early to run," she said, as the two of them began to slice through the cold morning air.

"Don't be. But thanks." Denny had gotten to know Suzanne some through the years since she had been married to Keith. Mostly through their shared love of running; like Denny, Suzanne had run competitively all through school growing up. Several years ago, Denny had driven from North Carolina to Pennsylvania to compete in the inaugural Runner's World race festival held in Bethlehem. All three of them had raced in all three races, which was aptly named the triple crown, and consisted of a five and ten-kilometer race that Saturday, followed by a half marathon Sunday. They all had roomed together in a hotel a couple of miles from the races.

Denny liked to wear a baseball cap, part of the race swag from the event, when he ran in warmer weather. Backwards, which felt much more comfortable on his head, as he was quite particular with the way any kind of article of clothing felt on him while running, especially his shoes, which he had the habit of tying and untying several times before any run, ostensibly to get the feel just right.

"This is the only time I can really go during the week," Suzanne said. "Plus, I usually have the whole trail to myself."

"Cool. No worries I have to log in by eight. But I've been running in the evenings."

"Yeah Keith said."

The two runners passed beneath the first of the town's two bridges that crossed over the Lehigh River. Denny throughout the years had several fragmented, illogical dreams involving these specific bridges; such as he'd be on the metal spans or supports underneath, trying to make his way across, or he'd be on the bridge itself in a car or bus, either by himself, or with some type of random collection of people he knew, or maybe didn't know. Or might have known?

His interest was immediately whet years ago when Trent had told him about the whole D&L Trail system, and described in detail where it traversed, and that yes in fact it did go underneath both of the bridges. On one of his trips up he had run it solo, all the way south and through the Lehigh Gap between the Blue Mountain, to the Nature Preserve building located downslope from the Appalachian Trail. The park ranger there happened to be an uncle of one of Denny's former cross-country teammates and had filled him on the network of single track trails recently hacked out on either side of the mountain, which connected up to the Appalachian Trail itself on the south face. There was even a ten-kilometer race held there in the fall.

Denny and Suzanne were now running on the dirt and gravel. "How's your running these days? Any big plans?"

The two of them continued on for several more strides, at a pace a little under nine minutes per mile. "Alright I guess," Suzanne responded. "So hard in the winter around here. And I hate treadmills. Keith can run on them but not me."

She was shorter in height, maybe five foot-three, and it was doubtful she had more than about five percent body fat. Or weighed more than a hundred pounds. Denny knew she was a tough, tenacious runner and quite competitive; but the type of runner and person who quietly and confidently goes about their work, and one whom it would be quite apropos to include the word humble, in any attempt to articulate the traits of their personality. A quality Denny admired, and wished he had more of himself.

"Yeah, I was never a big fan of treadmills," he replied. Though Denny imagined if he lived permanently in a northern climate he would become more acquainted with such machinery. In fact, he was almost drawn to the idea of them lately, as in his mind he had formed this picture of a treadmill in say a basement, that was also part of a makeshift home gym, and provided a kind of quasi romantic escape from the harsh, unforgiving tentacles of old man winter's firm, steely grip. Plus, it would break up the yearly training cycle a little more so.

"You picked a hell of a time to come up here," Suzanne said with a chuckle.

Denny returned with a hearty laugh, "I know, right! Guess I'm a fan of doing things the hard way. Or a fool. Jury is still out on this one." Across the river, visible through the tangled masses of bare tree branches, Denny caught sight of the light of the sun above the hills which languidly rolled back off to the east. He could hear the first wistful chirps of birds hidden in the woods, that climbed up and over the large, steep hills bordering right up against the near side of the trailway. Denny asked Suzanne if she had any upcoming races she was signed up for or was thinking about entering.

"I've got the Saint Luke's Half in March. Or wait, its early April. I'll probably do the Nazareth 10k this spring too. Ronnie and Nicky ran the 5k there last year."

"It's nice that your kids run."

"Well they like it. Sometimes."

"Weren't you first masters at Nazareth last year?" Denny loved to look up and pore over race results, which included those from eastern Pennsylvania. He would scroll through and inevitably find names of people he knew ran up here like Suzanne, or people whom he had run against in school.

"Third actually. They have grandmasters there too." Suzanne paused for a few moments, "which I will be at the next running of."

"And you don't look a day over thirty."

"Right. I wish could feel like I wasn't a day over thirty after a run. Now that would be sweet."

Denny ran hard some days. He started one of the five to fifteen-kilometer training plans in the Jack Daniel's book, even though he didn't necessarily have any specific time goal or target race in mind; but he liked the idea of incorporating some regimented running into all the mileage he was laying down. And this plan consisted of two or three harder workouts per week, and a long run-the remainder of the days were free to be filled in. All of which led to him feel like he was starting to catch fleeting, transitory hints of some sort of ethereal fourth dimension, which by its own oblique nature perhaps defied verbal description, though Denny assiduously attempted to articulate as best as he could in his ubiquitous notebook. The payoffs out on the road, he sensed, were beyond any numbers quantifiable on his beloved Garmin watch; this in fact all cut much deeper, like being enchanted by the faint touch of a cool summer breeze while drifting off to sleep. Or like being first introduced to a new philosophy or religion, or that euphoric burst one gets when first encountering a potential paramour. Whatever it was, and whatever was going on albeit transiently within, seemed to point towards distant horizons much more palatable to the eye, then some of those he had encountered much too often in his past. Enduring, not living, was the most accurate way he could describe such morose periods. "Bah. No one can explain all this, anyways right?" he asked a now familiar, neighborhood stray cat at the end of a run. Denny received a blank stare in reply.

That Saturday Denny met Keith and his son Ron at Castle Burgers, a small restaurant shaped like a chalet one would expect to come upon in say Switzerland. But it was located on First Street in Lehighton, right next to one of the bridges. Denny ordered the house specialty burger; a half pound of beef cooked to medium by choice, covered with sautéed onions, several strips of bacon, jalapeno peppers, pepper jack cheese, a smoky flavored barbecue relish, all topped off with a fried egg. The place had birch beer on tap, something he could never find down south, and furthermore no-one had ever heard of in the first place. Denny would attempt to describe the soda as a more earthy tasting root beer. He also asked for a cup of ranch dressing to dip his sweet potato fries in. Once they were all at the table, Denny took a couple fries in his hand, swirled them in the cup of dressing, then pointed the fries at Ron. "What say you, young man?"

"Nothing."

A few small drops of ranch dressing had fallen on the table. "What are they teaching these kids today in Junior High?" Denny asked Keith.

"Well it's actually middle school now."

"Oh? That changes everything then."

"What are you talking about?"

"I don't have the foggiest idea Ronnie. But it never seems to stop me." Denny took another bite into the juicy burger, and again allowed all the flavors to meld together inside his mouth in some sort of culinary dance, while being aware that his exaggerated, overt manner of purposeful eating was definitely drawing the attention of both his lunch companions, as they exchanged bemused glances.

Later in the lunch, Denny explained, "this is my one big cheat meal of the week. Truthfully it usually turns into a cheat day for me, though I'm not one to necessarily split hairs with people over it." Denny took a drink of birch beer and continued, "I'd probably be considered an outcast or interloper in some ultra conservative nutritional circles if they knew what I was up to."

"What the hell is he talking about?" Ron asked his father.

"Watch your language Ronald, we are in a public place," Denny quickly replied. They all laughed. Denny briefly thought about Andrea back down in North Carolina. And Xavier too. He wondered what they were up to on this Saturday. Probably teaching a fitness class. Or getting done by now. At least Andrea would be. He wondered too how much they had been running. Denny hadn't been keeping up a lot of contact with people outside of his small, current circle up north.

"I've been cutting back on sugar. Processed foods too, especially because of the salt. Or sodium. That's a big one for me since I have hyper tension, or so I've been told. This...," Denny made a sweeping motion with both his arms, then picked up two more fries and dipped them into the ranch dressing, "is referred to as a cheat meal by those with more knowledge on the subject than little 'ol Denny Defillipis here. You my friends are allowed one such meal per week." He ate the fries then leaned inward across the table and lowered his voice. "But as previously admitted at said table I fuzz it up and it turns into an entire day. Gives me more latitude for my transgressions."

"Where did you stumble into all of this?" Keith asked, while trying to suppress more laughter, albeit not too successfully.

"Excellent question. And Ron, don't get swept up into all of it. It may turn out to just be some sort of eccentric cult. Like scientology but involving food. Don't cut yourself off from nonbelievers, that would represent I would think a tipping point. You look like you are doing alright, still playing football?"

"Yep. And wrestling right now." Ron was built thicker like his Dad and was also on the muscular side as well. Last time Denny had seen him he had to have been less than half his current size.

"He's only lost a few matches this year. All that weight lifting is paying off," Keith said as he hit Ron on his forearm.

"I'm twelve and three."

"He's ranked fourth in the region at one thirty-six."

"Nice!"

"It'll help him for football too. Starts up in the spring again would you believe?"

"It's at the old high school field this year."

"What is?" Denny asked.

"Spring camp." Ron had already finished his burger and fries. He smiled at Denny who was still eating, and in the throes of savoring his meal. "So, you can't eat here again until next Saturday?" he asked.

"That's the discipline my friend."

Keith stood up and was putting on his jacket. "Come on Ronnie we've got to get out of here. Nicky has a basketball game at two."

"Tell her good luck."

"Will do amigo."

"Later," Ron added as he got up as well and followed Keith out the front door. A few minutes later Denny realized just how nice it had been to share a meal with others.

Denny laid down on his mattress with arms folded back under his head and stared up at the ceiling. A crack ran from the one wall and ended almost right above where his chest was. For some reason he hadn't noticed this until now. Denny laid there moving nary a muscle and thought back to the time he had met Keith at Baer Memorial after being on the road some nine, ten hours that particular day. It was a late July evening; Ron was attending pee-wee football camp, so Keith had said let's take a run around town. They had headed up the dirt road leading into the stadium, and then up the Ninth Street hill, as the sun indolently sagged downward through the hazy sky to the west, over the rolling farm country of Mahoning Township. It had felt so wild and weird that he was running through Lehighton, not twenty minutes after setting foot there for the first time in so many years. It had all come rushing back at him, giving him goose bumps even in the warm, humid air. Memories that is, like one big jumbled collage that couldn't be picked apart or sorted individually. He had felt almost as if he had crashed into a wellspring, buried ages ago somewhere within his consciousness.

Years later such feelings weren't nearly as conspicuous-the real enchantment lay in the virginal experience of return. Nonetheless, vestiges of it could still be stirred up, especially while on foot, though Denny seemed to sense that by necessity, all of it must have a certain shelf life; he suspected that if he hung around long enough expiration dates would eventually be reached. There was a certain level of nuance in all of this. At some point in the afternoon Denny drifted off for a short nap.

Chapter 3

Sunday morning Denny was awake real early, before dawn had even broke. The cold air inside had an effect no doubt on his awakening; the house was drafty, as most older, wooden homes are-when the temperatures plunged outdoors, Denny would feel the effects indoors as well, despite the fact that he would cloth himself in multiple layers. He had persuaded Keith a few days ago to set the thermostat up a degree or two (which was located downstairs in a separate apartment unit), though not without being given a breakdown on the cost of oil, and the voluminous quantity needed over the duration of a normal winter season just to keep the entire house modestly warm. Had Denny protested a bit further, he would have likely been reminded by Keith that was he was being granted free rent, and that he wasn't in North Carolina anymore.

Denny raised the blinds on the side window and peered outside, though he couldn't see much of anything yet at such an hour. A snowstorm was forecasted to strike the area with upwards of a foot of snow, depending on which prediction one looked at. Denny checked as many as he could on his phone, and on the radio as well, which he turned on low volume to an all-news am station as he sat back down on his mattress, with a hot mug of coffee cupped in both hands. Like he tried to do most mornings, he went through a mental list of things he was grateful for, which today included the pending snowfall, and the crazy idea he had come up with last night to embark on a super long run, this fine February day.

After methodically changing into running gear, Denny headed out the door to begin his epic escapade, which he decided to name the 1st Annual Carbon County Winter Ultra. Barring something quite unforeseen, he would be the only participant in this year's affair, but perhaps if success should smile upon him today, the event could expand going forward.

The air was raw, real raw and cold beneath a solid grey dome of clouds starting to become barely visible in the eastern sky, though it did not dampen the enthusiasm Denny had, as he took the first few steps on the sidewalk and on down South Second Street. The taste of snowfall was almost palpable, as he made his way up the steep hill on Fourth Street and into the big cemetery, where he followed some of the macadam pathways between rows of tombstones. There was a cross-country course the team had run on once, maybe twice, near East Stroudsburg, which went through a cemetery before ending on top of a big hill up a dirt road; Trent liked to bring up that course in conversation, for reasons Denny had never asked about, or never really thought much about, though it popped into his head this morning. Perhaps he was a fan of graveyards?

Denny began to warm up a little as he made his way through the slumbering town and started the long climb up Beaver Run Road and on up into the heights, though when he got beside the old football stadium and cinder track, he slipped in between the metal fence gates and entered the grounds. The track itself had lost some of its shape due to neglect; it was overgrown with grass along most of the outer perimeter, and there was a set of bleachers in the middle of what used to be turn three. Nevertheless, Denny for kicks turned two laps on the oval; his spring running home for the better part of ten years. He could almost feel the presence of numerous ghosts out there with him-apparitions of not only his younger selves, but of all sorts of past teammates and competitors too. Denny looked for the small wooden ticket booth that he used to duck into and temporarily hide after hard interval workouts, but it was likely long gone; he exited back out the gate, and back out onto the roads. Instinct told him not to linger too long. Besides which, he had a race to run.

Once up in the heights, Denny took a turn eastward and ran on the smaller, rolling hills along the first ridgeline, past the Ukrainian Homestead situated on several acres of property that was a mix of open fields and tracts of wooded land. There were several stone buildings scattered well back from the road, and a big in-ground pool a good hundred yards or so away. The place itself was always shrouded in mystery-this private enclave that no one seemed to know much of anything about, which was well marked along its vast perimeter with 'No Trespassing' signs. Back in school, one of the regular training runs went past the bottom part of the homestead and was referred to simply as the "Ukes run." And apparently it was still referred to as such from what Keith and Trent had told him.

Off to his right, through a clearing in the trees, Denny could see southward to the Blue Mountain, the top of which was becoming slowly blurred and erased by the lowering ceiling of now whitish, grey clouds, which looked like they were about to birth snowfall at any given moment. The wind had also increased slightly, sending an occasional shiver through Denny's body, though overall, he no longer felt as cold as he had when first beginning the run. He ran at a comfortable, easier pace, between eight and nine minutes per mile; he knew what lie ahead as Flagstaff Mountain loomed just off of his left shoulder, and that the mile plus trek to her top would require a healthy store of energy in reserve.

Plus, he was only about a quarter of the way into the planned run; he continued to monitor his physical body, in attempts to diagnose any kind of distress in its embryonic phase, in order to make any consequent adjustments to alleviate as best as possible any such ailments. Which was a necessity especially during longer runs. It seemed to Denny to be similar to what a race car driver did, constantly monitoring their cars. And like a race car driver, inherent risks were involved in pursuit of one's passions, which in Denny's case today was challenging himself to the longest run he had done in probably over two years, in the face of an impending winter storm. To those outside the fold, it made little sense.

The house that Kenny Sanders used to live in caught Denny's eye; a little abode tucked off a dirt road which dead ended by what would be corn fields in the summertime, that stretched several acres back to the woods behind the small Packerton Dam. Many an animated night was spent there as a teenager and college student drinking beer and liquor. Good times, Denny thought as he ran by, good times indeed. Then he added aloud, "Jack God bless you, you crazy son of a bitch." Jack was a tramp, an old vagabond who squatted for a while in a weathered, abandoned trailer parked at the edge of the fields. He would oft be spotted during the heat of a summer day walking the nearby roads carrying a case of beer from town, several miles away. No one knew where he came from, or where he eventually went; a peculiar image in the collective coming of age of Denny and friends. Perhaps as Denny kept running on by the universe grinned, for it's all one strange comedy anyway.

But there was nothing funny about the climb on foot up Flagstaff Mountain. The road was inclined at about thirty degrees, or so it seemed, as Denny began the measured ascent through the woods. But in all truth, he loved the challenge of it, taking the hill one piece at a time; the road corkscrewed around one turn after the other. As his legs filled with lactic acid Denny again remembered how he relished this terrain, and how he missed such runs such as he missed snow, which had now begun to lightly fall. What great timing he thought, as he wound upwards towards the summit, then crossed over a dirt parking lot in front of the night club which sat perched on the edge of a thousand foot, nearly vertical drop.

Denny stopped for a few moments to savor the view-way down below lie the town of Jim Thorpe, its houses and buildings appeared like little colored dots arranged in random, yet geometric patterns protruding outward from the Lehigh River, which looked like a thin blue string delicately dropped at the base of the gorge. The bridge which spanned the river, and connected the two parts of the town, was like a white stick lying on the ground. Denny figured he would be running across the bridge in another hour or so. The snow increased in intensity; Denny turned around and in-a-flash, began the descent back down the other side of the mountain. Plus, it got cold fast standing still.

When he got near the base of the mountain, Denny found the trailhead to the Switchback Trail, which cut its way through the woods to Mauch Chunk Lake. It was a hard-packed double-track, gravel trail; even in the winter the dense vegetation created a canopy like effect. The forest was a mixture of deciduous and coniferous trees; the trail extended almost parallel to a swift moving mountain stream, that made its way eastward toward the Lehigh River, through the murky, damp valley. Ferns and moss covered the floor of the woods in warmer months, which gave one the impression of stepping back into a more primitive environment, that has existed mostly undisturbed by the human race for thousands of years. Though the trail system and pathway were originally a gravity rail line used in the 1800s to transport coal and other minerals off the mountains.

Denny stopped running briefly and walked over to the stream. He took off his gloves, then bent down over the water with cupped hands and got himself a drink. It tasted cold and pure, and he appreciated the simplicity of taking a drink like his grandparents had taught him to do while out in nature. Denny wiped his hands dry on the front of his track pants and put his gloves back on, before heading back up the trail.

About two miles later there was a clearing in the woods near the one end of the lake; Denny could now see that the snow was falling at a steady, moderate clip, and had blanketed the ground with fresh white powder. Visibility had been reduced to about half of a mile, as he looked out at the frozen over lake. The weather could be very different in the span of only a few miles from where he grew up and was staying in Lehighton, to up here in the higher elevations only a few miles to the north. Winter generally kept a firmer grip here, something Denny recalled as the made his way through a meadow extending out from the east end of the lake, then up into another section of woods along the near shoreline. He glanced back to see his foot prints in the snow.

Denny emerged near the marina and swimming areas and followed the park's main entrance road out to and then across Lentz Road, where he picked up the next section of the Switchback Trail; a much tighter and much more technical single track that angled up and across the southern slope of the Broad Mountain. The snow was starting to stick to Denny's hat and gloves and was now covering the roads too; apparently the winter storm was arriving as advertised. But the woods again provided a bit of shelter from the elements, as Denny commenced the three-mile trek to the small town of Summit Hill, which would serve as the turnaround point in the ultra, and as the race's only official aid station.

When he was a kid, his Dad and some of his running buddies used to run the Switchback Scamper, a ten-kilometer race held in conjunction with the peak of fall foliage. The mountains would be awash in a blazing palette of reds, yellows, oranges; a striking testament to the autumnal artistry of mother nature. The race started and travelled through Summit Hill, then followed the trail downward that Denny was running now and finished near the lake. While his Dad and many others raced, Denny would hang out by the big pavilion which always had tables set up with chicken barbecue sandwiches and kegs of birch beer, and real beer too. Usually his Dad would place in his age group and pick up an award at the post race ceremony there.

As Denny picked his way up the trail, he recalled how good of a runner his Dad actually was or had been. The man could certainly flail himself to the point of utter exhaustion, as evidenced by his rather vocal, heavy breathing at the conclusion of races and runs. Perhaps Denny himself had inherited a little of that tolerance to pain, and the ability to push his athleticism to the brink? Who knew-it had been so long since they had even spoken, and all of that seemed so far gone and forgotten, like nothing more than cursory memories from a distant lifetime once lived. By now Denny was mostly inured to it all, though he became oddly aware for a few fleeting moments of how alone he was out there on the side of the mountain.

After what seemed like a much too lengthy, robust climb, the trail spilled out onto an asphalt road, with a couple of houses on the one side. Some cars were parked in front of homes; there was what looked like a fresh set of tire tracks form a big pickup truck that Denny ran by. It seemed like about two inches had accumulated so far. Denny had become aware somewhere back on the trail, in the middle of the dense woods, of how hungry he was, and that his body could use a boost of calories. And some more liquids couldn't hurt either. There was a gas station on the outskirts of the town that he planned to stop at; two boys traipsed by on the road, one of whom returned Denny's hello.

Finally, he made it to the Sunoco gas station and food mart. The town of Summit Hill had begun to assume the look of a winter wonder-land, which brought a smile to Denny's somewhat raw feeling face, for he missed seeing scenes like this; though as a car spun its tires and almost slid through an intersection, the problems and inconveniences of such serene looking weather were also duly noted.

Denny used his mouth to pull off one of his gloves and reached down into his short's pocket for the plastic zip lock bag containing paper money. He brushed some of the snow off his beanie and walked inside the warm store. "Morning ma'am. Quite the storm brewing?"

"Uh huh," mumbled the older, kind of frail looking lady wearing glasses behind the counter.

"Ran all the way here from Lehighton," Denny added as he walked down an aisle. He got no response, as he looked in vain for Clif Bars on the shelves, before finally grabbing two peanut butter almond PowerBars, and a twenty-ounce bottle of water from one of the coolers. An internal clock ticked inside Denny's head, though it was a bit silly since he wasn't actually being timed in this thing, like in an actual race. A burly guy in a heavy flannel coat and hunting cap trundled into the store; he went over to the coffee pots and poured himself a big cup. Denny could smell the coffee. Later he told himself, when you are back home. And keep moving. He thought of some scene or advice in a book about not sitting down on the chairs at aid stations, but the thought quickly vanished.

The store clerk asked the guy how the roads were, but he had little to report since he had just woken up a bit ago, and apparently could not be counted on to provide much information on that, or any subjects, until he had gotten some coffee into his system. Feeling like an outsider, Denny went up to the counter and paid for his food and drink, then added, "have a blessed day," on his way out the door, and on back out into the snowstorm, and the back half of his ultra-marathon.

He went over and stood by a cement wall behind a row of gas pumps and took a long drink of water and began eating one of the PowerBars. A few cars slowly churned along the road, perhaps taking its occupants to church services. He finished the food, which had a sweet taste, took another long drink of water before throwing the bottle and wrapper in a garbage can, then bid adieu to the aid station, and began the return journey home. It had taken him two hours and thirteen minutes to get there, and he had run a little under fourteen and a half miles. Denny felt fatigued, but nothing to be alarmed about as he got out from under the overhead shelter of the gas station, pulled his beanie snug down almost to the tops of his eyes, and headed out to the road.

He amused himself like a young lad following his own footprints but going in the opposite direction on down the road, or by alternating that with running in the tire tracks, as the thoughts of hot coffee twirled around in Denny's mind; before he knew it, he was in the woods again, back onto the trail. And then suddenly he was on the ground. It was a hard fall forward, though he did manage to get his arms out in front just enough to somewhat brace the impact. Denny laid still for a few seconds, a bit in shock, before he slowly stood up, hoping that he hadn't done any damage to his body. He took a few cautious steps; his legs seemed to be moving ok and still retained a normal range of mobility, though in his left side, especially the hip area, he could definitely feel the effects of the tumble. Denny's arms and upper torso seemed also to be okay, albeit a bit sore in spots too.

Having all the clothes on that he did had cushioned the blow and may have been his saving grace. Denny began to gingerly run again. He had fallen many times on the trails, the worst of which happened a few years ago during the Iron Mountain fifty miler, deep in the Appalachians of southwestern Virginia, when his foot clipped the top of a root just as he had begun really accelerating down a hill. That fall had snapped a wrist watch in half, bloodied up both legs, and left a nasty gash on the chin, all of which required a thorough cleansing with hydrogen peroxide at the end of the race. Which ironically was more painful than most of the race had been.

About twenty-five minutes later, Denny had descended the mountain, and after crossing over the main road again, he followed the same route taken on the outbound trip. By now the snow was coming down rather hard; big white flakes filled the sky and reduced the visibility to only a hundred or two hundred yards. Denny could barely make out the far shoreline of the lake. Plus, the wind had increased; for the most part the woods had provided a reprieve from. Denny heard the low rumble of a snow plow on the road; he watched the big yellow truck with orange flashing lights on top go on by. As he made his way back onto the lower part of the Switchback Trail, Denny was cognizant of how cold his face felt, and that his feet were pretty cold as well. Later he would think about what could have possibly happened if he would have been seriously hurt falling.

But this section of the trails was a welcome relief; Denny no longer had to be so attentive to footing like on the much more technical single track he had just run and fallen on. And once he got into a running rhythm, and was somewhat protected again from the weather, Denny slipped into sort of a meditative trance, whereby what could be best described as a euphoric sensation began flowing through him, making it seem as though his whole being was floating down the trail, with little energy or effort needed to sustain forward motion. Or as if a drug had been slipped into him-his thoughts, when they did occur, were soothing, amiable; but mostly he did not think at all, as the mind floated alongside the weightless body, as if suspended from the physical laws of gravity. Everything was crystalline pure.

Unfortunately, all good reveries must end, at least for those who aren't mystics or saints. As Denny neared the end of the trail he glanced at his watch; he had been running a 7:05 mile pace on auto-pilot, though the grade was slightly downhill. He had run over twenty miles; Denny calculated the rest of the route, which was down Lentz Road through the historic section of Jim Thorpe, catching the towpath back to Weissport, crossing the bridge into Lehighton and, then on up to the apartment. God willing should he make it, he will have covered close to thirty miles. The snow continued to come down steady and hard; once again Denny pulled his beanie down as far as it would go without obstructing his field of vision. And again, he became acutely aware of being cold, the kind of cold that permeates into every part of the human body. He knew he still had a lot of work to do, and for the first time since he had set forth, he began to question the decision to run so far.

The snow laying on the road had become a little more challenging to run on; it required a certain degree of effort by Denny to lift his legs up and out with each successive step. It helped to run where vehicles had left tire tracks, but there were just enough cars travelling along the road to force him to predominately stay off to the side, which was uneven in parts where the asphalt met the soft shoulder, all of which laid beneath a couple inches of snow. But once in town there would be sidewalks to run on which would alleviate some of these new concerns. Denny passed by a black Labrador retriever milling about in a yard adjacent to a house; "what's up boss?" he asked.

And into the historic quarter of town he ran, like a traveler finding civilization at last. Denny's legs were heavy and tired, his shoulders and neck ached, and the bottoms of his feet felt sore, yet onward he trekked. Long runs like this were tests not only of physical endurance, but mental fortitude, and stretched the bounds of the spirit to the breaking point, and perhaps beyond. One moment you're savoring the taste of peanut butter in your mouth and imagining the sizzling juices of a hot cooked steak, while the next you are sprawled on the ground berating yourself mercilessly for being so cavalier and careless with your footfalls, and for the naivety of thinking that a twenty-five, thirty-mile run in a snowstorm wouldn't be all that tough.

Mostly the machinations of change a runner encounters are more sublime and play themselves out over extended periods of time. Changes in terrain or weather, or things like cramps, blisters, strains, chafing, gastrointestinal problems alter one's physical well-being, which in turn affects the runner's temperament, and emotional well-being. Denny had only run a couple of ultras and two road marathons; he was a bit of a novice to all this world of extreme distance running-he had always been more of a mid-distance guy, focusing on the mile in track, 5000 meters in cross country, or five and ten-kilometer road races later as an adult. But he had read about the transcendent bliss that can appear after hours of running; something of which he had gotten a rudimentary taste of in his aforementioned running past. Perhaps out here, today, he'd be able to sample some of that sweet nectar from the running gods.

The metallic chiming of the bells of Saint Jerome's Church snapped Denny out of his train of thought; he looked over and saw several well-dressed parishioners trying to shield themselves from the snow, as they made their way up the front steps and on into the warmth of the sanctuary. Denny ran past the old opera house, which per the engraved sign above the front doors, had been open since 1887. And he ran by antique shops, small art galleries, book stores, cafes, and coffee houses in the quaint downtown. As a young couple walked out of a shop, Denny caught the aroma of coffee, mixed with the smell of freshly baked pastries, which kept afloat his spirits to complete the remaining legs of his adventure. He fumbled inside a pants pocket as he ran and pulled out the second PowerBar and ate it, just as he approached the county courthouse, nestled into the side of a hill across the street from the historic train station museum in the town's square.

Denny took a left at the courthouse, crossed the street and headed up the hill towards the bridge that would take him to the other side of the river, and eventually to the towpath. On the bridge, the sight of the heavy falling snow above the flowing waters of the river was like something out of a Bob Ross painting. Snow covered the larger exposed rocks above the surface of the water; the big white puffy flakes dissipated when they hit the river itself, while the surrounding mountains and trees were almost entirely coated with snow. This is a big part of why I do all of this Denny thought; he slowed the pace to revel in the scene's precious moments for as long as he could. Beauty born from suffering, or something like that he also noted to himself; sustenance for the inner life, and the artistic one too. He couldn’t quite put it all together, but he could feel love, and in kind returned heartfelt thanks as he exited off the bridge.

A half mile later Denny was smack up against the base of the mountain; he followed a dirt road next to the railroad tracks to a spot down river where he could cut on over to the towpath. The rock face dropped almost vertically the last few hundred feet of the mountain, though somehow trees managed to grow and hang over the side, which dumped more snow on Denny when the wind gusted. Years ago, he had come across a scene in the John dos Passos *USA* trilogy; two itinerant workers were making camp for the night along the river near where he ran, but the guys become so spooked at night, they ended up packing their gear and getting the hell out of there long before the first signs of the morning light.

Denny crossed the railroad tracks just past the water treatment plant, and after doubling back around he found the little path he was searching for, partially hidden by an opening in the trees. He had to slide down the small, steep hill on his backside until he got to level ground, and then found where he knew the end point of the towpath would be based on the gaps in vegetation, since it was not visible beneath the now several inches of snow that had accumulated.

He could really feel the toll the run had taken on his legs; they had a leaden, heavy feel to them, and his left hip from where he had gone down, was quite sore again. Also, his left Achilles tendon periodically throbbed in a fair amount of pain. Plus, the cumulative fatigue of the run had a debilitating effect on his overall body, which seemed to ache all over, especially in the neck and shoulders area. In summation, Denny was bush-wacked and exhausted; he had run almost a marathon and had been on his feet and for the most part moving, for the better part of four hours, and still had close to an hour left of running. "Fuck," he yelled as he slipped and almost fell again.

The road of excess leads to the palace of wisdom. William Blake popped into Denny's somewhat muddled brain a little bit further down the trail. In a clearing he gazed up at the snow-covered mountains on either side of him. "Though I walk in the valley of the shadow of death..." he said aloud but couldn't recall how the rest of it went. Denny thought about the book on Mysticism he was reading by Evelyn Underhill. William Blake had been mentioned. The doors of perception. Once the doors were cleansed man could glimpse infinity. Or something like that. Denny pondered this idea as he made his way under a railway trestle, which momentarily insulated him from the snow, and provided some snow-less ground to run on. Back out in the snow he slipped and almost fell again, but this time there was no reaction from Denny.

He wondered what Todd Hufnagle was up to. It had to have been ten years since he had last seen Huffy around these parts. Or more like fifteen? Maybe more than fifteen years. Denny used to send his mom Christmas cards; one year she had even sent one back. But he had stopped at some point. Why-he wasn't exactly sure? He wondered if she was still alive. No, that's crazy, she must still be alive. He would have heard about it from Jerry, or maybe Phil if she had passed. What a tender loving soul, Martha. Martha P Hufnagle. Denny laughed out loud. There was no 'P' in the name. That derived from Chris P. Jones. The 'P' that is. To set him apart from all the other Chris Joneses of the world. So, it had become an ongoing joke to insert the letter 'P' into peoples' names. Though there was a Chris T. Jones who played wide receiver for the Eagles. Seventy-two catches his rookie year. Was that right, and if so why did Denny recall that? He disappeared then. People do that. Denny had thought about disappearing many times. In a way that was what he was doing now. Celine always talked about escaping to a cabin in the woods. Like J.D. Salinger. Though he had written a few good books first. Denny wondered what Celine was up to. He felt a shudder up his spine as he suddenly felt really far away from people in North Carolina.

The snow continued to fall; at times it was almost a white out. Denny looked over to his right at the Lehigh River, the far side of which was barely visible. When the winds increased snow swirled in every direction, as if a child was furiously shaking one of those snow globes that apparently Denny was fond of. He seemed to be able to detach himself from his own thoughts and mind; able to peer in as if he were an outside observer. And when he did so he would refer to himself in the third person. Denny was damn near covered in snow; by now it was sticking to his waterproof jacket and pants as well, and his shoes were almost encrusted with a slushy mold of snow and ice. Frequently he would shake the snow off his head and body, but any kind of movement outside of what was essential to keep running forward seemed like wasted motion, draining whatever vital resources of energy he still had left.

The canal was iced over and covered with snow. The Pennsylvania State Game Commission would stock trout in it every spring, and usually his grandfather brought him there on opening day in April. There were also a lot of sunfish in the canal, or sunnies as everyone called them. They would hang in schools right near the edge of the water and bite at just about anything used for bait. Sunnies didn't put up much of a fight either once hooked, and never grew bigger than eight or ten inches in length. There were snapping turtles in the canal too; Denny hooked one once, but thought he had landed a big trout, and was disappointed when he started to reel in and saw that it was a turtle on the end of the line. His grandfather had to cut the line for him, in order to get the turtle off. Denny wondered if his grandfather knew he was thinking about him just then. And if so did it make him happy, and perchance was his grandmother there too?

Denny had had some regrets for how he had behaved as a grandson; he only ever knew one set of grandparents, since his Dad had been raised in a group foster home, having never known his own parents. Denny had gotten into this awful habit of saying things under his breath purposefully, like calling his grandfather an old fool, just to see if he could actually hear him. He never once did respond, but had apparently heard all of the mean, stupid things Denny had been saying. Sure, he was just a kid, maybe seven, eight years old and kids do a lot of mean, stupid things for no reason, but years later after his death it still would occasionally bother Denny, though he had been taught through grace to be absolved of such wrongdoings, if one was repentant for their transgressions.

A couple of tears welled up inside Denny's eyes, and trickled down his frozen face. "I'm sorry. I'm sorry," he said softly into the falling snow. He felt meek and really small as he trudged forward, step after painful step. Sometimes everything can feel so drab, dreary, almost hopeless. We come, we go-so what? Blah. Bah humbug. "What are you all looking at?" he hollered at a group of mallard ducks huddled under the overhanging branches of some trees on the far side of the canal. None of them bothered to respond. Perhaps they were too cold to extend the effort. Or they thought he was just nuts, which Denny knew to be true. It was all becoming clear to him as he made his way southward, with head hung low to try and keep from constantly having to wipe precipitation from his face.

Denny ran for a while and tried hard to just not think of anything at all. He concentrated intently on the sound of his feet hitting the ground, one after the other, one after the other. He started saying to himself left, right, left, right, left, right-matching the cadence he was running at. Denny pictured being back inside the apartment, sitting up close to the radiator, with a hot cup of coffee in his hands. Perhaps an open book in his lap, or he'd bring the radio into that second room and listen to some music, as he watched the snow continue to come down. Like on those first days he was up here. That had been rather peaceful. Maybe things weren't so bad after all; he had just hit a rough patch in the run, that's all. Thoughts weren't real things, anyhow right?

As he came upon part of the towpath that was much closer to the river, the sound of the water rushing on through the snow-covered rocks attracted Denny's attention. He listened as intently as he could to the pulsating, ululating sounds emanating towards him, which created a gentle, symphonic harmony, filtered through the faint, hushed noise created by all the snowflakes landing on the trees and the ground. The sound would ever so slightly change as Denny moved, as mother nature continually altered her tune, rising the tone a bit and holding it for a few brief moments, as if suspended on an invisible beam, then dipping back down an octave, before quickly rising back up again. While the quiet, steady rat-ta-tat-ta-tat-ta-tat-ta of the landing snow seemed to keep time. A crow called out as it took flight from one of the trees between the canal and the river; Denny watched the large black bird circle around inside the spin wheel of snow, until he lost sight of it somewhere across the river.

Before he knew it, Denny was at the trailhead of the towpath. He felt a twinge of nostalgic sadness that his one-man ultra-marathon was about to reach its conclusion. He was still very cold, and exhausted throughout every fiber of his being. He was hungry again, and thirsty too; but none of it was cause for much concern. Denny felt joy radiating from his heart as he made his way back onto the roads, through the village of Weissport, up and over the bridge back to the other side of the Lehigh River one final time, then up the steep two block hill on Bridge Street, down one side street, and finally back down South Second Street to the front of the house and the finish line.

A car slowly drove past, navigating its way carefully through all the snow. Denny smiled and waved to the driver, to whom he did not know. He hit the stop button on his watch, and eagerly checked the finally tallies. 28.64 miles run, in the time of 4:39:16. Denny pointed skyward and gave thanks, before dragging himself up the snowy steps, carrying the imaginary first place trophy he had won, back on inside to the confines of the dry, warm apartment.

Later that evening Denny walked down to Keith and Suzanne's house; he guessed the storm had dumped over a foot of snow. School would definitely be closed tomorrow, and depending on how bad the drifting was, the next day as well. Denny had to sort of high step his way down the sidewalks since nobody had shoveled yet. Snow continued to lightly fall from the dark nighttime sky, as if mother nature was putting the final, intricate touches on another wintry masterpiece of hers. For now, the winds had subsided, but were forecast to really pick up again later, and into tomorrow, in conjunction with a bitter cold air mass coming from Canada, behind the storm. The last couple weeks of relatively mild winter weather was coming to a screeching, abrupt halt. A guy across the street was shoveling his car out and said hello to Denny while taking a momentary break and leaning on his snow shovel. "Looks like it's about done with," he said.

Keith and Denny went out to the garage and up into the room above, which was filled with more things then one could ever imagine getting in there. Most of which were games and toys the kids played with or used to play with; it all seemed to be indiscriminately scattered about the long, rectangular room. Denny ached all over and felt every one of the stairs, primarily in his quadriceps and lower back, but it was one of those good achy feelings reminding him of what he had accomplished today. Suzanne stayed inside the house, confounded, and perhaps debating just how demented Denny actually was, though he suspected deep down she was also a bit envious of his extreme exploits. A part of us all, secretly desires to walk a mile in the shoes of a madman; some of us are just better at hiding it than others. Denny figured he'd sleep like a baby tonight too.

The two of them, Keith and Denny that is, got into a game of ping-pong, much like they used to play in college at the house Denny resided at for two years off campus. One of the guys he lived with had converted an old dining room table into a ping pong table, which led to many a late-night marathon bout of games, after the bars had closed downtown. Some of these were punctuated with highlights including valiant dives across the floor, or crashes through the swinging door that led into the kitchen; heroic efforts to return shots and sustain hotly contested volleys.

Keith had bought an actual table and set it up in the garage, though he admitted that he didn't play too much, nor did the kids much either. They seemed to be more into the electronic hoop shoot game set back up against the one wall. Keith won the first game rather easily, then set his paddle down on the table. Neither of them made any diving attempts either; Denny would have likely torn a muscle. "Dam I don't want to work tomorrow. Maybe I'll just go for a twenty-eight-mile run of my own," Keith said with a laugh, though it sounded a bit forced.

"Maybe you'll be shut."

"Doesn't matter," he quickly countered. "I'll have to work from home."

"Oh, gotcha." Denny knew Keith wasn't happy, though to what depths he didn't know. It was one of the tradeoffs Denny had made years ago when he moved south, which put certain measures of distance between close friendships, such as the one he shared with Keith. It was a tradeoff he accepted, and over the course of the years Denny drifted apart from some people, while he remained closer with others. There were old friends he realized that he might not ever see again, and people that if he did, it would be merely a product of chance. And the world had changed in the last fifteen years as to how we all stayed in touch and remained connected; phone calls and in-depth conversations had for the most part been replaced with text messages and following social media updates. It was much easier for things to fall through the cracks.

"I'm fucking miserable," Keith said as he chucked a ping pong ball off the table. It bounced pretty hard then hit a window on the side wall, ricocheted off the top of a television, then fell to the ground and bounced a few times, before settling into a roll until its momentum was finally exhausted, and the little white ball came to a stop about six inches from Denny's feet. He slowly bent over and picked up the plastic ball and looked closely at it in his hand, as if he could divine some kind of wise and appropriate response from it.

Keith continued, "maybe it's just this job. Everything though really. I don't freaking know. Just all so depressing right now." Denny didn't say anything as his friend paused for a few seconds, then added, "I feel like I've busted my ass for nothing. Well not nothing. But what's the use. We are just going to get bought out in six months. Or maybe a year."

"By whom?"

Keith forced a wry laugh again. "By of all people in the world Mitt Romney's company. Bain. You remember all that during the election?"

"Of course."

"They're acquiring five or six travel companies like us and then going to align them all under one system." Keith worked as a software developer for a company in Bethlehem. He continued, "then the cuts will come. I'll get to engage in the process of doing the very work which will lead to the elimination of my position, sooner rather than later if we all do a good job."

"That son of a bitch. For the record I did not vote from him."

"Me either. What irony too. But the place has sucked for years. The atmosphere of it, which is so typical of your quote on quote corporate American work places. I won't bore you with all the specifics. Probably be over for me soon anyway." Keith looked around on the floor, presumably for another ping pong ball, but instead picked up an orange, rubber mini basketball from the hoop shoot game. Denny wondered if he was going to throw that too.

"Always so much with the kids. And Suzanne completely stressed out too. Thought same thing was going to happen where she worked but may have dodged the bullet. At least for now."

"That's a relief."

"Yeah I don't know. We'll see." Keith was bouncing the ball as he spoke, but it hit his foot and rolled under the table. "Ron has been getting into fights at school. Some kids trying to bully him. Acting strange and they don't want to be around."

"That sucks. Seemed okay to me."

"And Nicole says she is depressed or something. One night we found her in the bathroom with all kinds of knives out. Suzanne is going to take her to a psychologist this week. Ronnie doesn't help the matter either by making fun of her. But I really got on him the other night about it. Has to be a better big brother and help out around here. Suzanne just went into the bedroom, shut the door and cried."

Denny wasn't sure what to say, though he did offer to help out in any way he could, and also suggested the two of them get out for a run soon.

"Let's get out one night this week. Maybe after some of this weather lets up."

"Sounds good."

"Come by the old high school in the evening, Ronnie has wrestling practice there and I can slip out."

"Sounds good my man."

Keith seemed to perk up some as he picked his ping pong paddle back up from the table and said, "let me see how much I can kick your ass again in another game."

Denny walked around to his end of the table and picked up his paddle as well. It was just like old times, sort of.

Chapter 4

A few evenings later Denny got all bundled up and headed out on foot to the old high school gymnasium to meet Keith. As predicted, the days and nights had turned much colder since the big snow storm, though not atypical for this time of year. But it had turned outdoor runs into much more of a challenge, first of which was getting enough clothes on to stave off the bitter elements. Denny had taken off the last two days, to allow his legs and body to recover from his big weekend foray.

Once outside and running, he had to be really careful of ice, especially on the sidewalks, which would accrue melted snow and ice during the day's sunlight, that would quickly refreeze once darkness began to settle in. Though as he set out on South Second Street, the childlike sense of adventure he felt Sunday returned; Denny made his way around snow piles that seemed to be lined up in every direction he attempted to run. But as he got onto Iron Street, which was much wider, Denny found that running on the road itself was easier, though he still had to be wary of patches of ice and snow. And it was cold, bone chilling cold, though fortunately the winds had mostly subsided.

Denny made it to the parking lot in just under twelve minutes, but he didn't see Keith outside, so he decided to walk into the lobby and warm up for a few moments. Welcome home champ he thought to himself, as he walked through the two sets of glass doors, properly noting that he could still amuse himself by punching up his long since forgotten legacy a few notches.

"What's so funny?" A female voice surprised him.

"Damn. Jennifer Merluzzi."

"Sure is!" Denny stood transfixed, bewildered and somewhat dumfounded as to how to react. Fortunately, Jennifer quickly added, "well aren't you going to come over here and give me a hug?"

They embraced in the middle of the lobby. She felt soft, electric to the touch, despite all the layers of clothing Denny was wearing. He hadn't see her in... he had no idea. In actually he did but couldn't think of it right then and there.

"What the hell are you doing here?" A playful hit on the arm accompanied the query, and Denny was aware that he suddenly felt rather flushed, though the contrast in temperatures was rather extreme.

"Uh I'm meeting Keith to run. Keith Druckenmiller. He's an old friend of mine. That lives here. Anyhow he's in here somewhere, at least I think he is and we are going to go for a run." Wow, I sound like an idiot Denny thought, as he rubbed the beanie on his head like he had lice in his hair.

"Maybe I know him. He run all the time like you?" Denny noticed that her emerald green eyes had a radiant glow and bore into him when she spoke. All the familiar features were there too like the long, flowing sandy brown hair, that naturally fell over her tall, slender body. The slight tilt of the head when she spoke, while her hands instinctually pushed back her hair behind her ears. But most of all it was the wide, beaming smile; a smile which in its stunning silence promised that everything was alright, and would be, regardless of what vicissitudes life pitches our collective ways.

"Well I'm trying to get him to run more but I would term it a work in progress right now. I'm pleasantly surprised my running proclivities have filtered up to these parts?"

"Hey I see some of the pictures on-line. Run Denny run!" Jennifer laughed, then looked him right in the eyes again, and added in a slightly more serious tone, "but that's really awesome. I'm so happy for you."

Denny was beginning to get his legs under him. "I'm so remiss, where are my manners? How are you-god it's been so long. Your kids are here wrestling, right?"

"Jake is. Toby is running around somewhere. Probably getting into trouble."

Denny saw Keith out of his peripheral vision coming through the open gym doors and heading across the lobby towards them.

"He's thirteen now, Jake. Loves wrestling. Last year he made it pretty far into the state meet. Finished sixth in his division. Or weight I think they call it."

"Weight class."

"Yes." She playfully punched Denny in the arm again just as Keith strolled up.

"Wow leave Denny alone for five minutes in a school," Keith cracked as he put a Penn State beanie on his head.

"Yeah right? I mean I'm just out here minding my own business and this joker comes over." Jennifer smiled at Denny.

"Sounds like our Denny."

"Oh, this is Jennifer. Jennifer this is Keith. I don't think she knows who you are which is quite odd considering your reputation around these parts." They all shared in some good-natured laughter, though Denny sensed he was fidgeting a bit. He wanted to stay right there and talk to Jennifer, but he also kind of wanted to get out of there and leave off on a high note.

"Hi Keith. It's a pleasure to meet you," said Jennifer as she smiled and extended an arm towards him. "I hear you are going to keep good company with Denny out there in the cold tonight."

"Well it all depends on what he has in mind?"

"Okay folks we are getting side tracked here and this is an educational facility." The open roads were beckoning, and were the place that Denny felt most comfortable, even when it was fifteen degrees out. Plus, he didn't want it to all slip; he started to turn towards the glass doors back across the lobby.

"So good to see you Denny," Jennifer said, as she seemed to sense what he was thinking as well. And Denny thought he heard a little something in her voice, a twinge or slight variation of tone, which when combined with the gleam in her eyes, made him think that he needed to say something more, and quick. His heart seemed to be beating a bit faster, for his pulse had quickened.

"You as well Jennifer. And hopefully it won't be another ten, twenty years until our next encounter."

"Well I'm here every Tuesday, Wednesday, and Thursday evening."

"Oh, do you have a kid who wrestles too?" Keith asked.

"Yeppers. Jake. He loves it."

"Jake Schoenenberger?"

"Guilty as charged."

"That's one of Ron's friends. That's my son."

"Cool beans!"

Denny and Keith headed through the doors and into the frigid, winter night. Denny's Garmin had timed out while inside, so he had to stand there and wait until he reacquired a satellite signal again. Keith jumped up and down to try and stay warm. "She seems nice," he said between bounds, and telling him to hurry it up. "I'm pretty sure I have seen her around."

"Man, that takes me back," replied Denny as they headed out of the parking lot and took a left turn down Beaver Run Road towards the old football stadium. As the stadium and track came into full view, Denny continued, "I ran some laps in there a bit ago. Brought back some good memories. Army Track Keith, we were a dominant force in the eighties. Three-peated under the tutelage of the legendary coach Richard Miller."

"So, who's Jennifer?"

The moon was almost full as it hung like a bright yellowish white ball suspended in the oily black sky, which stretched out in every direction above the town as they ran. Stars glistened all around, and looked so far off and so very cold, like bright little icy dots arranged in an ink blotter splattered across the panoramic view, well above the houses and tree tops. The stillness and serenity of the night was almost tangible; sometimes when Denny was out running he felt like a millionaire, surrounded by all the currency he could ever possibly need.

"She's a girl I used to know. Many, many years ago," Denny finally answered, unintentionally in rhyme. Experience, the hard won and bitter kind, had taught him a measure of emotional temperance when it came to encounters with the fairer sex.

Especially when such emotions went deeper, and beyond the mere superficial. Keith sensed this and knew Denny well enough to recognize when he was a bit clouded in the head by a woman. Something of which certainly he would attempt to take full advantage of, for who doesn't enjoy seeing a good friend squirm just a tad bit?

As they turned onto Mahoning Street and headed west Keith said, "well could you elucidate, a little further," with an unmistakable air of mischievousness in his voice. "If nothing else, I could use a little distraction..." Denny had picked the pace up early, a bit on purpose. Keith was breathing harder, but it didn't stop him from continuing, "...from the miserable monotony. That has become. My life. Give me some, details, for goodness sake!"

Denny had to leap over a snow pile he saw at the last instant; the street lights on the road were spaced out and pretty dim. He almost slipped and fell when his left foot landed on more hard-packed snow and ice, but he regained his composure after several strides and said, "well when you put it in such terms, I'd be happy to attempt to oblige."

The two runners passed the new high school grounds and sprawling complex of buildings, on the land that used to be the county fairgrounds, and also the location of the cross-country course Denny ran on in school. "We hung out a lot the summer after my first year in college. Eventually started dating. She had an apartment above a garage on the alleyway behind Third Street. Down off Coal Street." Denny had cut the pace as they rounded Hientzleman's curve, named for the meat market there. It was a dangerous stretch of road infamous for many car accidents. He flashed back to an image of her coming home late in the day from nursing school; it didn't seem like that much had changed with her since then. Besides a marriage, and two kids. But he was almost positive she was divorced, and she hadn't been wearing a ring.

"And?"

"Oh sorry. I got distracted."

"It's refreshing to see some things never change."

"The long and the short of it, if I may instead just summarize the whole thing, is that I was madly in love with her. She was, as they say, the one."

"I vaguely recall you mentioning her once or twice."

"She actually came and stayed with me for a while at Penn State. Before we started hanging out. When I was living on Beaver Avenue."

"With Ed and Kenny"

"Yes, Kenny was gone by then. After his father died."

They turned onto Selwyn Road, which was a series of short rolling hills along the far side of the school grounds. As the last hill was crested, the sound of the Mahoning Creek became audible; it flowed beneath a small bridge just before the intersection with Bridge Street. Straight ahead was the municipal pool, and beyond that the park which contained Baer Memorial field. In the dim light cast by the moon, and the pale glow of some scattered street lights, the park looked like an idyllic winter-scene fit to adorn the front of holiday greeting card. Except for the gurgling sound of flowing water, everything was dead silent.

"I regretted it for a long time after we broke up. Or to be truthful she got tired of me and moved on. Which I can't fault her for. I never liked to talk about it much back then. Was like poking at a festering wound. But that was a long time ago."

"I hear ya."

As they headed back into the residential part of town, Denny filled Keith in a little more on some of the substance he could remember about her, and about the two of them. The pain of it all had thankfully been removed a long time ago, and it was a sweet sight indeed to see Jennifer in of all places, the lobby of the school they had spent a chunk of their most impressionable years in. Yes, it was kind of surreal Denny had to admit. "Maybe you guys can get back together?" Keith said to him just before they began the tough climb up South Seventh Street.

"Gee that never crossed my mind." Neither of them felt the necessity to acknowledge the lie, perhaps as a result of having to focus on the incline in front of them. The pace slowed considerably as Keith's breathing became fairly labored. Left to his own, Denny may have attacked the hill, but he had caught himself before being an ass in trying to run too hard for Keith for selfish reasons. Finally, they got up near the Grove Park, where the road leveled off some.

"Man, I'll tell ya," Keith started, as his breathing had become a little less pronounced. "I miss this. Getting out here like this. Feels good."

"Yes, it does."

"Gotta get back. Into a routine. Just so beat up of late. Mentally."

"Yes, physically you seem alright. More hill running will certainly help matters."

Keith laughed. "I'm just out of shape. Hills are fine."

They crossed over Mahoning Street, which unofficially demarcated the center of town, and was one of the main travelled roads connecting the east and west ends. Then the climbing began again, which caused Keith to slow the pace considerably. Denny fell into a slow stride beside him and figured it may be a good time to at least attempt to proffer some advice or share some more of his ramblings about running and life, which if nothing else, could serve as a partial distraction to his comrade.

"I feel your pain, I do." Denny thought of Bill Clinton and wished he had said the words impersonating the former president's voice, something he once liked to do. "I wish I could say or do more to help you and the family. I know from what you've been saying, especially of late, that you feel defeated. Or trapped. Spinning in circles with very little hope, or not much of a chance to enjoy much of anything." Denny wasn't sure where he was going with any of this, but he carried forth, after catching his breath too. He could feel the toll the hills were taking on his legs as well. "Or you have no good options. Stuck. I've been there. Of course, under much different circumstances. And we all have varying responsibilities and obligations. And desires. Dreams. Things we would like to see go in certain ways." Denny fell silent again, as he feared he was making little sense. Keith's pace had slowed to a crawl, as the hill was unrelenting. He looked and sounded a bit distressed.

"For sure," he gasped between breaths.

"I thought I was going to die several years ago. A miserable drunkard. Drug addict. But as my presence here tonight should prove, I did not. Then a few years ago when Rayanne left all the life seemed to get sucked out of me. Didn't want to get out of bed. I left a good paying job when I thought my anger and misery could cause me to snap."

Denny took in some air, like a seasoned saxophone player as they neared the top of the hill. He could feel the music building inside of him to a crescendo; the sounds of their sneakers hitting the macadam kept the beat. "But the one thing that was always there for me was the running. No matter what. Like a parent who loved me unconditionally. And it's just as true today, maybe even more so. I don't know what the answers are for you like I don't know what they are for myself. But out here all of that doesn't seem to matter quite as much." Just as the two of them were about to finally summit the hill, Denny concluded his oratory. "I guess what it boils down to Keith, is this is where you could say that I find God."

Lactic acid had flooded Keith's legs; evidenced by his gait and demeanor as they turned right onto Coal Street, and mercifully onto a slight decline. Denny looked out ahead and thought he could just barely make out the rolling hills about two miles to the east, across the valley basin through which the Lehigh River flowed. It reminded him of the time he was running in Albany, New York, when as if by magic suddenly a panoramic view of the Hudson River Valley became visible to him ahead in the distance. All the miles, all the places; that familiar, warm joy welling up inside.

Keith spoke then, and said, "I don't know man. I hear what you are saying. That's great and all. I guess I'm much too cynical and down to buy any of the God stuff right now."

That night Denny took out his notebook and sat on the floor in the empty room. He lit a candle too and made himself a cup of hot green tea and added a teaspoon of honey from a jar that Celine had gotten him for Christmas; he took mindful little sips from the cup like he had read in a D. T. Suzuki book years ago. Denny flipped through the notebook's pages, reading some of the things he had written, skipping through others. Thoughts jotted down, ideas; maybe it would all lead somewhere, maybe it wouldn't. Whispers on the wind; temporary, lilting ethereal tugs on the soul's strings. The words were also an escape-Denny knew he could only fool himself up to a point in believing that they weren't. But language could also be a vehicle that took him places never imagined. Places that perhaps, represent the jumping off points, to what is not readily discernable or communicable. An old friend once gave him two pieces of advice; write about what you know, and most importantly, write for yourself.

Once he was at dinner on a date with a girl named Diana; she asked him if he was running towards something, or away from something? After a pause, and some thought, Denny replied that it was likely a combination of both. They only went out maybe one or two more times; Denny suspected that she had quickly grown tired of him incessantly talking about running.

Chapter 5

Suzanne had told him about an upcoming 5k race on the D&L Trail and added that she would even try to convince Keith to run it as well, though Denny was dubious about that. He pulled the race flyer up on-line and checked out the details; the last time he had competed in anything official here must have been whenever the last track meet was his senior year in high school. I'll get Trent to run this fucker too he thought, while grabbing his car keys and heading out the apartment door.

Denny was getting very familiar with the area again. Not that he had to relearn his way around or had forgotten the lay of the land so to speak. Rather it was the kind of familiarity one acquires when in the same general place for any length of time, in that they become quite attuned to, and sort of internalize all the peculiarities which when taken together, weave a tapestry that defines any locality, big or small. And all of this served to at times fill Denny's head with foreboding thoughts of immanent doom, or perhaps better described, and in less egregious terms, he would get this strong sense that he didn't belong there anymore, and therefore should leave back out as soon as it was feasible to do so. Which in actuality, could be accomplished at a moment's notice. He had gotten a text message from Jennifer right as he was pulling the car out onto the road but chose not to read it as he headed out to Trent's.

"You should coach Army Track."

"That would be cool. Following in the footsteps of Richard Miller." Trent and Denny still talked after all these year almost reverentially about their first coach. Ironically Trent was now married to one of his nieces, though Jill had grown up participating on one of the rival teams named Navy in the town's Booster Club Track and Field program. Which still existed today, with the same named four teams.

Trent had gathered and set the balls on the pool table located on one side of the two-car garage. He paused before breaking and leaned on his cue stick. "What time does the race start? I have to be at work by ten, ten thirty at the latest. Lots of deliveries and my Dad can't lift that much anymore."

"Gun goes off at nine son."

"Rats." He picked the stick back up and broke the pool balls; nothing went in. Denny got up from his seat on one of the weight benches on the other side of the garage. There was also a universal in there, an array of free weights, and a treadmill over in one of the corners closest to the interior of the house. Trent and his steps sons used the equipment a lot, though his teenage daughter barely set foot out there. It was kind of cold in the garage; the only source of heat was from two portable heaters, but Denny dug the functional simplicity of it all. And Trent loved the place; the house was the same house he grew up in and had been sold to him by his parents a couple years ago when they moved to be closer to the used furniture store they owned, about twenty miles away.

After circling the table a few times, then finally missing the shot he took, Denny said, "well if you're not going to go to the race it gives me a chance at winning it."

Trent set his beer can down and said, "I doubt I could break twenty-one, or even twenty-two. At least right now."

"Winter in PA. Yes, yes."

"I've been riding her pretty good though," Trent said as he pointed his cue stick at the treadmill.

Denny looked at the treadmill with a touch of jealousy, and with a certain discernable degree of lust in his running heart. Again, he had that bizarre, romantic feeling; as if such a dalliance with one of those machines could perhaps satisfy some hidden fantasy buried deep within. Or maybe it was nothing more than the timeless idea of wanting what we cannot have, or that the grass always seemed to be greener on the other side? Though the former didn't quite make sense, since he could always find a treadmill such as in this garage to run on, or at one of the local gyms. But that would be somewhat different than having his own set up like Trent did, waging his own private battles against the winter season, raging on outside the window, a scant few feet from where he ran. Logging the miles; casually dreaming about warmer weather to come in the months ahead.

"That's what's nice about North Carolina. I can train fairly uninterrupted through the winters if I choose to, instead of this survival like running half the time up here. Though I do miss the snow. I trained for two marathons during the winter down there." Denny took his shot and sank a ball, then moved to the other side of the table and eyed up his next play. "It can be cold though, and windy. Winds off the ocean in the winter can cut you to ribbons. But not like here. Don't get me wrong." He made another shot.

"I remember the wind in Portugal off the ocean was nuts sometimes. But I mainly golfed then. Not much running."

"You were defending our country." Denny finally missed.

"True. No problems on my watch. Wonder if Shoemaker is running Saturday?"

"Funny I ran into her when I was out running last weekend. Or the one before. Way out 902. We ran together for a bit. She's training for the Pocono Marathon this spring."

"I see her on the D&L sometimes." Carla had been in the same class as the two of them, but didn't run track or cross country in school, taking up the sport later in life. She was a pretty dang good runner.

"She looked strong. Was going fourteen miles. At a decent pace too."

"Puts me to shame," Trent said after he sank another shot.

"You also raise pigeons that can race."

"True." Trent missed, and walked over to the full-sized refrigerator and pulled out another can of beer. "Not too many people can say they do that..." he cracked the beer open and took a drink, "and run too."

"You're a true Renaissance man."

The morning of the race Denny awoke early. It was still pitch-black outside as he stepped out the door and onto the little landing atop the stairs. It was quite cold as expected, about twenty degrees, but there was little to no discernable wind blowing, which was much more of a concern. Running hard or racing when it's cold out is tough but manageable; but when the cold is coupled with wind, conditions become nearly intolerable. Denny's body involuntarily shivered, so he closed the door and went into the kitchen to make coffee. A few minutes later he carried the mug down the hallway and sat back down on the mattress and whispered “oh my” into the still, silent room. This should be interesting Denny thought, as the coffee began to warm his insides.

He pulled into the D&L parking lot, which by now he was fairly accustomed to doing, and checked his phone for the time which was 8:12, or forty-eight minutes and counting until the start of the race. Several people were gathered under the pavilion by the picnic tables. Denny took his time getting out of the car, then slowly walked over to pick up his race packet and bib; he wanted to savor all the attendant details of the day's experience. On occasion over the years he had thought about how cool it would be to run a race back in his old hometown, back where this whole running odyssey had begun a few decades ago. It was another one of those enigmatic reverberations that he liked to pursue; which possibly contained intimations of some indiscernible world. That, and it gave him something productive to do, if nothing else.

"Dee-fill-ip-iss, comma Denny," he enunciated to one of the women all bundled up and standing behind a picnic table that had a pile of race bibs and paper forms setting on top.

“Yes, the one from North Carolina. Good morning!" she exclaimed rather pleasantly, while finding his name on a sheet listing all the runners. "Came along way for this one?"

"Wouldn't have missed it," he replied as he picked out four safety pins from a small box. While he was being handed his bib and race t-shirt Denny explained that he had grown up around there, Franklin Township to be exact, but had moved away a long time ago.

"Well we are glad you are here," one of the other volunteers chimed in.

"Me too," Denny replied, as he turned and headed back over to his car. He saw Suzanne heading towards the pavilion, and she must have known what he was thinking for she said, "he's still sleeping. I tried to wake him but he just grunted and rolled over."

"Ahhh."

"Let me grab my bib and we'll go for a warm-up run. I'm freezing."

"Sounds good."

Denny popped open the rear hatch of the Rav4 and sat inside to change his shoes. Even though it was less than a five-minute drive to the start of the race, out of a superstitious habit, he never wore the running shoes he was going to wear in a race while in route. An older pair of Saucony Virratas were chosen for today's affair. They still had pink laces in them from the Run for the Tata's 5k Race in Wilmington last October; a big breast cancer fundraiser in North Carolina. He hadn't worn them since then, as the tread was about done, but he still loved the lightweight, pillow-like feel on his feet. Suzanne walked over as he was tying the second shoe. Carla was with her as well.

"Nice shoes, very stylish," she said.

"Hi Carla." Denny hopped out of the back and closed the door. He kept on long pants and a heavy sweatshirt for now. "I enjoy making a fashion statement when I run with the public at large."

"Let's go. It's freezing out here," Suzanne said. She was bobbing around with her hands clasped between her legs like a school girl who had to pee.

Denny grinned and said, "lead the way."

The three of them headed southward on the D&L. The sun was out, and thankfully had begun the slow climb into the eastern sky, which helped obviate some of the cold. Denny made a mental note when they passed under the first bridge that it was almost exactly a half mile from there back to where the start/finish line would be. He knew that this section of the trail-way had been utilized over the years for various five-kilometer races, which were logically set up as out and back courses. One of the benefits is that the race would be free from any vehicular interference, and it also drastically cut down on the number of turns, though Denny wasn't a big fan of out and back routes. "Usually there's just a big orange cone at the turn around spot," Suzanne said in response to one of his questions.

The macadam part of the D&L was clear; it had obviously been plowed based on the fact that there was a continuous mound of snow and ice still remaining off to the one side. But once they got to the gravel section, which was also kept predominately in the shade by the Mahoning Mountain immediately off to the west, the ground had a layer of hard packed snow on top. Denny ran several steps onto; it didn't seem too problematic, and was pockmarked by human and dog footprints, though he agreed with his companions that racing on it might prove to be an interesting challenge.

"Well I'm just going to tempo it. I've got sixteen tomorrow," Carla said.

"I'll stay out of the snow until I have to," added Suzanne.

As they ran back towards the start, Denny told Carla he was a bit envious of her long run, and the fact that she was well into an extended training plan, working towards a big race. Though the flipside, and acknowledged by all, was not being tied into having to do a long run every weekend. The three of them chatted away amicably as they passed back underneath the bridges. Suzanne and Carla were convinced that Denny would win, which he attempted to downplay, while adding that he was fairly certain the two of them would be amongst the top three females, in what would most certainly be a small field of well under a hundred runners. Though as they made their way around the long sweeping bend, it looked like a lot more people had since shown up. Denny started to get the proverbial butterflies in the stomach as he watched a rudimentary finish line chute being constructed and caught site of a rectangular electronic clock being mounted atop a metal tripod.

And it was at times like this that Denny felt very much alive. Alive and viscerally aware of the passing minutes, on down to the seconds, which had the effect of increasing the intensities of not only the physical surroundings perceived by the senses, but the thoughts, feelings, emotions within were also magnified. He could almost feel the thumping of his heartbeat as he popped open the back of the car again and took off his outer garments. This may be some nondescript race in some nondescript town, but it was a race nonetheless, and every bit as important to all those who would toe the line here to test their mettle and fortitude, regardless if the goal was to win, place, set a PR, or just finish. Perhaps it'll be someone's first race? We all have our reasons. We all have our stories. Denny closed the hatch and slid his keys behind one of the tires. He smiled to himself as he stood up, thinking again of the beginning of the music video "Smugglers Blues," when Glen Fry's partner tries to assuage his anxiety by saying, "relax man, it's just a job."

Denny slowly jogged over to a lone port-a-john, located up past the pavilion. He had stripped down to shorts, a long sleeve Tec shirt, with one of his Cape Fear Flyer's coaches' shirts overtop. He would also wear a pair of gloves and a beanie to retain some warmth on his extremities. The port-a-john was freezing cold and abysmal, but a necessary stop shortly before any race. He knocked out a few quick striders back behind everyone; as he finished the last one Denny thought about the young men and women he coached and wished some of them were there today. It was always more fun going to races with some of the kids, and fellow coaches. He tapped the front of the t-shirt a few times, then made his way near the front of the assembled mass of runners.

A few moments later they were greeted by the race timer who reviewed some fairly standard pre-race details. The guy who was named Joe then introduced a lady named Barbara from the local Lions Club chapter, whom the race proceeds were benefitting. She explained that the monies raised would be going to help renovate a homeless shelter on First Street, which had been closed the last two years after the building had been condemned due to its lack of structural integrity. As she spoke Denny causally glanced about him and surmised that a few of the guys looked like decent runners. Carla stood right behind him and was fiddling with her watch, while Suzanne was off to his left and a couple feet behind.

It was kind of odd not to know more people at the start line of a race. A recording of the national anthem was played; it was a tape of a girl singing before a high school football game last fall. She was a member of the school's orchestral club. Denny wasn't aware until now that such a club existed, as he held his beanie firmly against his chest with his right arm. Wow, she has an amazing voice he thought to himself. After the tape ended, Joe authoritatively told everyone the race would begin in precisely thirty seconds; there was some nervous chatter and obligatory good lucks exchanged, which Denny said to Carla and Suzanne, though Suzanne did not hear him. He looked back and guessed there were about sixty to seventy runners lined up.

With a loud, shrill shriek form a bullhorn the race was underway, and the runners were off. Denny liked to script the first mile of a shorter race, whereby he would formulate a plan and try to stick with it notwithstanding how he felt, and what the field around him was doing. The idea was borrowed from football, and how the offense some games chose beforehand a set order of plays to run, independent of what the defense was doing on the opposite side of the ball. Denny wasn't quite sure what his current fitness level was, though his running had been solid, especially considering it was early in the season. His weekly mileage was averaging in the fifties, and he had begun doing some of the workouts in the Jack Daniel's book. Therefore, he had settled on a target of 6:00 to 6:05 for the first mile, and then hoped to negative split the last two miles. But that was before he saw that most of mile two would be on a snow pack, so he adjusted the plan to try and negative split the second half of the race.

About two hundred meters in, Denny checked his watch; he was running at a 5:50 pace. A little too hot he said to himself, though the pace did not feel too fast, perhaps a good early indicator. Three guys were ahead of him, the first two by a good twenty, thirty meters already. Denny guessed that they had probably gone out too fast, albeit he had no idea who they were, and what they were capable of racing a 5k in. There was a local kid Keith had told him about, Marshfield, who was a seventeen-minute 5k runner on the high school cross-country team, but based off the physical description provided, he was not one of the two leaders.

In the earlier stages of the race, Denny tried to soak up some of the significance of the event. Twenty some years had passed; almost too much to fully fathom, as it was about half the time he had been alive. Since then he had taken a journey he never would have imagined-in the words of Alice in Chains, "no one plans to take the path that brings you lower." Grunge, and the whole Seattle music scene, exploded and had become wildly popular about the time Denny would have last raced here; several of its heroes were long since dead, tragic byproducts of some of the same excesses he so regularly had also indulged in. Why some of us make it and others don't is a riddle inside the mind of God. The pain

Denny put himself through while running perhaps served as a subconscious reminder of a life once lived. But this kind of pain was laced with joy, not perpetual despair. This was celebrated and sought, not condemned and misunderstood.

Five-kilometer races become real tough really quick; racing them requires a runner to red line almost the whole thing. There is no settling in, such as in longer races. No, here it gradually, almost imperceptibly continues to require more physiological effort to maintain one's pace. Denny had moved into third place, and the runner who was currently in second place was coming back to him fairly rapidly. He knew he'd be ahead of him by the mile mark, which he was, as he went through in 5:57, before hitting the snow and ice pack a little way up onto the gravel part of the trail. Periodic glances forward allowed Denny to calculate when he might catch up to the race leader, as that gap was closing too.

And Denny relished the chance in races where tactical decisions could be a factor. Runners could be like chess players, making moves early for the sake of luring a competitor to respond, in such a way they might not have done otherwise. All of which could play into an overall strategy, bore out over the duration of the race. Then again, many runners ran solely for time, and blocked out what was going on around them. Or in a given race, a runner may simply be trying to execute a specific race or training plan, which may or may not take into account what others were or weren't doing, like Carla this morning. It was all part of the fun of it; the rules were simple-go from point A to point B, and your result is the time it took you to do so, and the order in which you got there. There were no stoppages in play, timeouts, substitutions; as a runner you are essentially on your own, amongst a crowd of people all on their own as well. It was one of the reasons why there was such abundant camaraderie in the collective suffering the sport produced, as we all make our way towards the same finish line.

The lead runner was now only about ten, fifteen meters ahead; Denny wanted to catch him by the turnaround. He would do that, then run behind him until the two-mile mark, at which point he would pass by and hopefully open a nice little gap, then hold onto the pace hard and hang on, diminishing any thought his fellow competitor may have of staying with him and challenging for the victory. Get to that bridge and the half mile mark, from there you know you can survive and make it. All of that seemed so very far off, as Denny concentrated on his footing.

The snow notwithstanding, he was also in the part of a race that can be a waste land. By now Denny had been running over eight minutes at a pace around his VO2max; sustainable yes, but the toil is starting to be much more intensely felt. The runner knows they have a lot more work ahead of them, which begins to seem quite diabolical in lieu of the stress saturating the body. These are the points where many a race goes to pot; the killing fields, which can take down even the toughest of us on any given day. Race enough and it'll happen, regardless of age, ability, mental toughness, running IQ-you name it. And it won't show the slightest trace of mercy or compassion as it sticks its fangs into the runner and buries them. Not today, Denny told himself, not today, as he stalked his prey through the shadows stretched across the snow-covered trail.

As they approached the orange cone in the center of the trail, Denny was just a few strides behind the leader; they briefly locked eyes when passing by each other. Denny gingerly went around the cone like a tap dancer way up on the front of his feet, then took several quick, hard strides to close up right behind the young man, who didn't seem to be breathing all that hard. Denny had also glanced at his watch which read 9:19. No other runner was close by.

The pace seemed to slow a half click from what Denny had been running, after he had followed behind for a quarter mile or so. Carla passed by on the left and said, "Go Denny," which he returned with a quick flick of his wrist and wave. She looked like she was in cruise control and was apparently well ahead of the next female. Suzanne passed by about fifty meters later, and also said, "go Denny." Though he didn't process it at the time, it was nice to be encouraged and cheered on by friends in the running community he currently found himself a part of, as he sat just off the race leader's shoulder. He wished them god speed and was rooting for them to both fare well.

As the two leaders ran past the far end of the fenced in municipal water authority's property, Denny guessed they were about 1.75 miles into the race; instead of waiting for the two-mile mark, he decided to make his move and pass, being fairly confident that a faster pace could be sustained, and that his competitor would not come with him. Like he was taught in his budding days of running, Denny laid his intentions bare as he went around the young man swiftly and kept his foot on the accelerator for another good fifty, sixty meters. The sound of foot steps behind him slowly faded, validating the merits of the move.

Denny was alone, delightfully alone, and in the lead when his watch beeped indicating the two-mile mark, just as a woman racer headed outbound whooped and hollered something about him being in the lead. Had Denny not been under such an acute strain, he may have enjoyed the moment a little more, but like most things which occur in a race through the prism of a hazy blur, it would be recalled later quite vividly; in fact, Denny got to speak to the woman after the race, who as it turned out was a volunteer with the Lions Club.

Back on the macadam pathway it was easier to run again. Though lactic acid was taking its menacing toll, especially on

Denny's legs, he was able to run through his burst, and settle back into a more controlled, hard race pace. He was entering into the point of a foot race where runners commence to experience the "bag of nails in the chest;" an apt, poignant phrase coined by the writer Alan Silistoe in *The Loneliness of the Long-Distance Runner.* Like the protagonist in the seminal story, Denny was in the lead. But unlike the troubled, hardscrabble teen, Denny had reasons today to win, if for nothing else, that at that juncture in the race, he could.

For the time being, Denny dared not take any furtive, backward glances; he wanted to, and needed to run with a healthy fear of being caught. There was still work to be done, he couldn't fall on the ball, or run the clock out. He also knew he had a solid time going and would finish with a good result if he could just keep his shit together for another few minutes. Life for now was broken into tenth-of-a-mile intervals, though exact measurements were not sought. Keep cool, maintain, Denny told himself. Make anyone bleed it out of themselves if they are going to catch you, like Prefontaine would say. Give them no quarter. Zeppelin. He would have to tell Trent about that later. "Focus!" He heard Andrea's voice loud and clear in his head. She would remind him of that at practices, and meets, for Denny was prone to pontificate, drift. In conversations. In life. He breathed in short, quick rapid breaths; that invisible threshold in the race where Denny could be sure he was going to make it had yet to be crossed.

Denny wasn't any kind of superstar runner, though he was good enough to have found himself in the lead, not only in some scholastic races, but a few road races as an adult as well. Smaller, local events-nonetheless he had notched a few first-place podium finishes. Those experiences had revealed that as a runner Denny ran hardest and could seemingly withstand almost intolerable levels of pain when he was in the lead. For when in the lead, one becomes the hunted, the pursued, and no runner worth their salt wants to ever get caught from behind, it's almost too wretched to even ponder. Most would sooner choke on the bile and drop dead, then let such a fate befall them. This morning Denny had the chance to play the hero in his own tender little drama; the stage props were arranged just so.

And he could see the bridge coming towards him. That confounded bridge. He was under it for a few seconds then back out into the clear; as Denny started rounding the sweeping bend of the D&L Trail, his eyes caught sight of the old folks hi-rise building that had stood there on First Street since he was a young kid. It was by far the tallest structure in the town, maybe twelve stories high, and for several moments its mere presence transfixed Denny, as if it had illuminated something deep inside his psyche; perhaps it was some kind of symbol beyond the scope of anything that could be objectively understood. Once he had started to write a story, which began with the main character standing on the roof of this very building, contemplating ending their life with one big leap. But this fictional person instead climbed on back down, though what happened after that remained a mystery, as Denny had never finished penning the tale.

The finish line was now visible up ahead; a quick look back revealed that no one was even close on the course. Denny could relax, somewhat, in the last four-hundred meters of the race. His legs were almost a bit wobbly, and the bag of nails wanted to explode through his chest, but there was pleasure in his heart, speckled with a little pride for good measure, as Denny was able to mentally absorb the rad fact that he was going to win the race. As he got closer, he could hear some cheers coming from the small crowd gathered near the finishing area; finally, he could make out the electronic red numbers of the clock ticking the seconds off, at a little over eighteen minutes. One voice in particular was clearly audible just up ahead; it was that of Jennifer's, as she yelled, "yay Denny!"

He strode hard the last thirty, forty meters as he approached two people holding a thin yellow ribbon in front of the chute. The last few strides were painful, but Denny didn't really feel them as he ran through the tape-the clock read 18:23. He slowed into a walk, with his hands grabbing his knees, then his hips, as he attempted to suck in some oxygen out of the thinner, winter air. Jennifer was waiting for him at the end of the chute, and Denny sort of let himself go limp as he put one arm around her shoulders.

"Holy crap you won!" she said, as he leaned in and kissed her on the cheek. "Of course, I figured you would," she excitedly added.

"I'm glad. I could deliver. On your lofty expectations. Of me." Denny grinned devilishly at her; some of the feeling was coming back into his body as they slowly walked away from the finish line area. He grabbed a bottle of water from an open case setting on the ground and took a long drink while glancing around the place. A strong sense of gratitude welled up inside of him; he gave himself a few brief moments to relish the morning's exploits.

"Let's head back and wait for Carla and Suzanne to finish."

"Sure thing."

"And thanks so much for stopping down. Road races are not the greatest. Of spectator sports." Denny took his free arm and put it around Jennifer's waist, pulling her close as he spoke. He was feeling a little confident.

"You can show your appreciation by taking me to dinner tonight."

Denny smiled. "It's a date."

A few other runners had come through the finish line, and Denny could see Carla just up ahead. She finished as the top overall woman. "Looks like a sweep for the class of '92 out here this morning."

"Aren't you freezing?" Jennifer asked.

"I'll throw on some clothes in a minute. Here comes Suzanne." Denny yelled up ahead to her, "finish strong Suzanne," as she approached the end of the race, and as the second overall female. Props to her he thought, I know how she hates this cold weather.

"Aaaahhheee back to the car woman. You were right I am freezing," Denny said to Jennifer.

At the small awards ceremony back under the pavilion, Denny was given a medal with the Lion's logo superimposed over the top of a silhouette of a runner, with the words 'First Place Overall Male' written beneath. He looked closely at the medal and thought about his Mom. Of late she had been on his mind more, probably in part because he was back up here in the section of eastern Pennsylvania she had spent her whole life in.

She appeared in a vivid dream a couple of nights ago; standing on the front stoop of their old house, calling him to come in for dinner. Denny could hear her from where he was at, somewhere not too far off, perhaps over in one of the neighbors' yards, but that part of it all was fuzzy. He didn't answer or call back to her; instead he just stayed still, so he could hear her call out his name again, as if he wanted nothing more than to listen to the sound of her voice as long as he could. Until her voice, and the dream, receded away and was gone. Later he had thought about what Xavier had once told him about dreams; they were the vehicle used by the departed to communicate with those still living. Perhaps that was the case indeed, he thought again as he got back inside his meager quarters and set his backpack down on the mattress. "What the hell am I doing?" he asked, but no one was there to respond.

Later that evening, after darkness had cloaked the town yet again, Denny headed out the door, down the steps and out onto the quiet streets. It was a clear night, and already quite cold as he made his way on foot up South Second Street in route to Jennifer's house, a few blocks away. The night sky was awash in stars; the moon at about a quarter crescent, cast nothing but the faintest glow down upon the alleyway next to Tommy's Rum Runners Bar. Noise from the barroom drifted out from the building; Denny used to drink underage in their back when the place was called BH's Bar. They had a happy hour every Monday and Thursday evening from 6:30 to 8:00pm. Thirty-five cent Schmidt's drafts was what him, Ed and Joey would drink on those summer nights, before heading over to the Grove to see what else was happening in town. Ironically that was about the same time he and Jennifer started hanging out, and eventually hooking up romantically. They hadn't really known each other much in school or had ever really talked, at least in any meaningful sense.

Denny asked Trent what he knew about her, but then kind of cut him off before he could say too much, as he thought perhaps it's best not to really know too much. Though Trent did manage to say that he didn't really know too much about her anyway, except that her one son was a pretty good wrestler, and in the same grade as Cody, Jill's oldest son. And yes, she did look pretty good the times he saw her over at their old gymnasium. Welcome to small town America, Denny mused to himself, oh how I missed thee. Just up ahead was the cemetery; his pulse quivered slightly, and his stomach lightly churned. He would be arriving at his destination shortly. Be cool, he whispered to himself, be cool.

Jennifer lived in half of a double home, with a large portioned porch in the front of the older house; a pretty typical looking home in Lehighton. Denny bounded up the three steps onto her side of the front porch and without any hesitation rang the doorbell. He heard, "comminnnggg," from inside, as he shook his hands at his sides, and tried not to peer through the window of the front door.

"Well good evening Mr. Defillipis, do come on in!"

"Good evening beautiful," Denny said as he stepped through the doorway and hugged Jennifer, once again giving her a soft kiss on the cheek. She looked radiant in the light of the house, which gave her hair a golden glow as it naturally cascaded down over a purple sweater she was wearing, which hung down over a pair of blue jeans tucked into brown leather boots just below her knees. The effect of which made her appear a bit taller, maybe just two inches shorter then Denny, who felt a bit conscious of how his own attire of khaki trousers and a button down collared shirt looked, though he did leave the shirt untucked.

"So, this is home. Well it has been for the past three years or so." Jennifer made a sweeping motion with her one arm as they both slowly moved through the living room. Denny was comforted somewhat in that his date seemed a bit nervous too; Jennifer kept flicking her hair back with her hands, which was a quite charming habit of hers. The television was turned to a local newscast. The weather was airing and the meteorologist was standing outside, which Denny instantly recognized as WNEP's backyard forecast.

"Oh, wow I used to watch this all the time! Do they still have Tom Clark on?"

Jennifer raised her eyes up in a bemused countenance. "Yes," she said with a laugh, as she touched his arm. "He's usually on during the week." Denny felt a surge of electricity course through him, just as he had felt when he saw her in the lobby. And there was that luminescent sparkle in her eyes, like a light cutting through the fog, guiding a vessel to safe harbor. It was all so wild, ecstatic, new and fresh-Denny felt like a school boy again.

"You have a lovely place here." The arrangement of a sofa and reclining chair, with a large coffee table in front of, gave the downstairs a comfortable, homey feel. There was a dining area in the next room, then a swinging beige wooden door that presumably led to the kitchen.

"It's not the Ritz Carlton but it will do. They boys like it. Though they hated it when we first moved here." Denny knew there were many more details behind such commentary, that at some point perhaps in the not too distant future would be discussed, but now certainly was not the time. He had had his own marriage dissolve as well.

"I'll show you the kitchen and the sun room which I really dig."

"Lead the way."

Indeed, he could see why she dug the sun room, or urban sanctuary as she referred to it. A back door off the kitchen led onto an enclosed porch, the top half of which consisted of windows partially covered by various hanging plants which gave the room a greenhouse like vibe, complete with a small tree planted in a big flower pot, sitting in the one corner. "It's a lemon tree. Believe it or not we got some lemons from it last year. In the summer we put it outside." A wooden bookshelf filled with books stood back up against the far wall; I guess she's still a reader Denny surmised.

"Nice!" he did exclaim aloud. "Hell, I could just live out here."

"Are you looking to move?"

Denny caught her eyes as the question seemed to take on a physical dimension of its own, and hover there in the room for what seemed like a short eternity. He could see that there was much more to the question, much more likely then Jennifer intended at the moment, but sometimes things just kind of come out, and when they do much deeper subjects are broached that don't have readily available answers, at least not any truthful ones in the present time. Since there are too many unknown variables in the matter being brought dangerously close to the surface. It's like capturing a momentary snapshot of another's subconscious, their secret desires and wishes, that perhaps they cannot even articulate, or are aware of themselves. For it's a bit too risky; our hearts have a wonderful way of being able to temper themselves just enough when some grain of prudence appears to be the safer and wiser route to take. Denny took a few small steps and took both of Jennifer's hands in his, then slowly drew her into him and kissed her on the mouth, the only way he could think to respond.

"HI," she said, in a voice they both had long since forgotten.

The streets were again tranquil save for a few passing cars, and one older gentleman walking his dog who passed by the two of them, as they walked up to Angelo's Italian Restaurant. Denny had never been there; it had opened after he had left, though he had heard over the years that it was run by some of the Fentilini family who also owned Dominic's Pizza, and another Italian restaurant in Jim Thorpe. For as long as he could recall there were always rumors that the family had mob ties all the way back to Sicily, and that here in the States there were connections to illicit enterprises involving gambling and drugs, though no one had even been arrested. However, many persons also subscribed to the theory that all of it was just a marketing ruse anyway to draw business into their establishments, since it added a side of intrigue to patron's meals, not easily found in such small-town environs. Plus, the food was always damn good. And as Denny held the door open for Jennifer, they were greeted with the aroma of garlic, and a medley of other wonderful smells, contained within the walls of the old converted house. He was famished too.

They were led to a table by the hostess; as they walked towards the back of the main dining area several people at a lively table recognized Jennifer and called her over. It was a party of seven or eight adults, and one young girl. Denny noticed a couple bottles of wine on the table as one of the ladies stood up and gave Jennifer a big hug. Apparently, she was a friend of her mother's, and also two of her cousins were at the table as well, though Denny was a bit confused on some of it as they were all randomly introduced to him, including the young girl who was named Ella. She smiled real big and said, "hi Denny," which amused him, and helped ease a bit of the nervous tension he suddenly felt with so many eyes on him.

"What's good to eat here?" he leaned down and quietly asked Ella.

"Pizza!" she exclaimed, before taking another bite out of the slice on the plate in front of her.

It was a surrealistic kaleidoscope of weekend night life in Lehighton that simultaneously piqued Denny's interest in human sociability, while again bringing to the fore nagging germs of doubt as to just what he was doing there to begin with. Though he had learned a long time ago how to live with conflicting interests and diametrically opposed ideas; wasn't it F. Scott Fitzgerald who said something to the effect that it was a mark of intelligence to simultaneously hold opposing thoughts? Besides which, if he was going to follow these bizarre notions percolating inside, such scenes as this, and their attendant stimuli, were going to have to be walked through. Denny would have to act as his own tarot reader and attempt to make sense of each new card as it was turned over. He couldn't afford to duck any of it, for that would detract from the whole of perhaps what he sought, thus undermining the full scope of the endeavor. No, if he was going to continue on with his vision quest he had to be all in, though he got a bit squeamish when it directly involved others.

He and Jennifer sat down at a table. "Margie's been working doubles and hasn't been out in like three weeks. And it's just like Frank and Shirley to get her half lit at dinner."

"They seem to be enjoying themselves. Ella says the pizza is good."

"Oh, it is Denny. We get it sometimes on Friday nights after football games or Saturdays after wrestling matches."

"Funny when we were kids growing up every Friday night was pizza night. We would switch it around between Pizza Hut or Dom's. Or maybe the Fire Company in Franklin Township if they were selling pizzas."

"Buuttt, I don't want you to think I just feed my kids pizza and butterscotch crème krimpets most of the time. I know what you must be thinking their mister healthy eater with all that running you do."

"Dam I used to love those krimpets! They still make them?"

"Sure. Any gas station probably has them. Or you can buy them by the box at Giant. Or any supermarket."

"You mean Lanes?"

"Lanes! God Denny are you back in 1987?" Jennifer exclaimed as she broke off a piece of bread out of a loaf in the basket placed on their table. She then poured some greenish, yellow olive oil on a small plate and swirled the bread in it. "Try it on this oil, it's delicious," she said as she handed him the clear glass bottle. "Have I ever steered you wrong?"

Jennifer was certainly correct. The bread was warm to the touch and absorbed the olive oil like a sponge, and it all tasted sweet, like there was a hint of basil or thyme?

"I think it's rosemary actually that gives it that subtle little pop," Jennifer answered, as she broke off more bread.

"So, what are you reading these days? I didn't have a chance to check out much of your library."

"Oh man it's embarrassing. Well not really. Lately I've been into this Finnish author who writes romance novels but are sort of like travel books too. With mysteries in them. I don't know how to describe it. Truthfully I haven't even read one in a bit anyhow."

Denny responded, "hey we all go through phases with what we are into right?"

"Oh, you remember that *On the Road* copy we were all reading and passing around? You, me, Jerry, Huffy. I forget who else."

"Heck yeah! Wow, those were some crazy times."

"They sure were." The last word out of Jennifer's mouth dropped slightly in tone as it rolled off her tongue. The times were crazy alright, but not always crazy good. Denny picked up on the vibe too, as he suddenly remembered the time he threw a bunch of empty beer bottles threw an apartment window in a spasmodic fit of anger; anger that ultimately was with himself. At the time he didn't realize how dangerously depressed he was, though in those rare, clearer moments he was aware of just how frightened he was that he couldn't comprehend what was going on inside of himself, intuitively seeming to realize that intense bouts of wretched misery, accompanied with foreboding feelings of hopelessness that caused him to morbidly contemplate things like what it would be like to stick a kitchen knife through his chest, or purposely crash a car at high speeds to make it appear as an accident, were not the norm for a young man in his twenties, who on the surface had all of his needs being met. The things that were helping him to maintain, cope, were in a cruel twist of irony the accelerants pushing him further down a spiral into the abyss. And he wasn't necessarily blind to what effects this had on others close by, like Jennifer at the time. Still, he was powerless to stop it. "Jennifer," he timorously began "I'm so..."

"No Denny," Jennifer abruptly interrupted. "I know you must have had it rough. Though I'm a little curious as to what all happened."

Just then the waiter came over to the table. He was a young, good looking kid with slicked back black hair, and a slight accent as he spoke. Another "family" member Denny suspected. He introduced himself as Anthony and with a fixed, serious demeanor asked the two diners if they would like any drinks and appetizers.

"Yes. We'll take an order of calamari," Jennifer told him. "You like that right?" she turned and asked Denny.

"I do."

Anthony wrote on his pad. He was quite muscular as well, and looked like he might be a football player, or someone who just liked to lift a lot of weights. He was probably about sixteen; his facial expressions gave away nothing.

"It doesn't bother you if I get some wine?"

"No not at all."

"Are you sure?" she asked with a quizzical look.

"Positive," Denny assured her. He looked up at Anthony and said, "I'm with the temperance league." The young waiter did not bat an eye.

This time it was Denny's turn to break off a piece of bread and swirl it around some more olive oil that he poured on a plate, while Jennifer intently watched. "Well two things ultimately happened. One, it was bad. Two, it got even worse. But I won't inundate you with all the details over such a fine wonderful dinner we are about to share. Jennifer, I am truly sorry you got caught up in some of it. If there is anything I can ever do to make up for it please tell me. I know I wasn't too easy to be around."

"There isn't. But thank you. Do you remember Concrete Blond?"

Denny thought for a few seconds. "Oh, the band? Sort of."

"Well they had this song called 'Joey.' A little after the time we were together."

"Sing it."

"Goodness no." Jennifer laughed. "I can't carry a tune. Anyhow it's about this guy drinking and she sings this lyric, 'I just stand back and let you fight your secret war.' It always made me think of you and I would get so unhappy and worried. But I heard many years ago that you really turned it around. I'm so glad." Jennifer reached her hand across the table and put it on top of his.

Denny squeezed her hand tight and responded, "me too."

Anthony returned with a plate full of calamari which was steaming, and a bowl of marinara sauce, which was also sweet and contained a strong hint of garlic according to Jennifer. After a few seemingly well-timed moments, Anthony asked the two of them if they were ready to order. Denny apologized, he hadn't even really looked at the menu yet, which surprised himself. "I'll be ready in three minutes," he announced.

Jennifer had already told him that she was going to get the pasta penne with mussels, and a tossed salad with the house dressing, that she explained to Denny was like a cross between a creamy Italian dressing, and a light vinaigrette. The way she could articulate details caused Denny's heart to flutter. "Excuse me," he said to her as he opened the menu back up, "but I have work to do."

"Try some of these calamari while you read. Or I'll eat it all."

The entire meal was simply divine, as was the time Denny and Jennifer spent together talking and laughing through the evening. Had one been a casual observer of their table, it would have been guessed that the two of them had been together for quite some time. It felt that way to Denny at least; all the years that had passed seemed to have melted away, and at one point he even made a toast, "here's looking at ya kid," as their glasses clinked together in harmony. Yes, the vestiges of that first love they had shared were still there; they ordered cannolis to go and headed back into the cold night holding hands and walking close together back to Jennifer's house. Denny spent the night there; Jennifer fell asleep in his arms as he waxed poetically about life by the ocean. "When the moon reflects off the waves as they unravel from the pitch-black horizon, a million diamond like sparkles scatter to the salty breezes..."

The next morning, she left him a fresh brewed pot of hazelnut flavored coffee on the kitchen counter, after giving him a kiss on the forehead before heading to the hospital for an early shift. There was a hand-written note on the counter top propped up against a mug. It read, "I'll smile every time I think of you today." Denny smiled too as he folded the note and slipped it into his pocket. He poured himself a cup of coffee and headed into the sun room, just as the sun's rays were starting to rise above the eastern horizon and bathe the room in a warm, radiant light.

Sundays were long run days for Denny, and today was no different even though he had raced yesterday. His hamstrings were quite sore and a bit stiff, which was to be expected, and his left calf was a little tender, but he figured all of that would gradually work itself out once he got part way into the run. The plan was to go for two hours, as suggested by his new friend Jack Daniels on weekly long runs. Denny also liked the alteration of doing some runs based upon elapsed time, rather than distance. Something of which he had done in the past as well, but it served now to add some freshness to the training being done, which was usually a good thing. He wondered where Carla was running, but then remembered she had said she was going to head way out Mahoning Street since it was clear of snow off the sides of the road.

Denny decided to head himself into Franklin Township, his true ancestral home, as he liked to refer to it. Long runs too, were Denny's unique little way of “following Jesus into the desert”, like some of the ascetic, spiritual seekers who lived many centuries ago. To an extent, he felt an affiliation with some of these religious wanderers. For we all searching he reasoned while lacing up his shoes, which bore the scars from his own pilgrimages of late. The sun had already begun to warm up the air, at least relative to the fact that it was still late winter. But enough so that Denny decided to strip off his long pants as he stood on the landing atop the stairway, and just go with shorts.

"Ow ow ow ow," he mumbled aloud as he took the first few strides on South Second Street. Denny's legs were pretty beat up, but they also served as a pleasant reminder of what he had accomplished yesterday, which he had not thought about much at all since his evening and night with Jennifer. He smiled inwardly as he slowly ran past Tommy's, then headed down hill to snake his way along a couple of side streets which would lead him to the first bridge across the Lehigh River. When he got on top of the bridge Denny looked down at the D&L Trail with a sense of satisfaction, though cognizant that he should temper his ego some. But just for today, he would bask in a little earned glory, for one never knows when the pendulum will swing.

Denny decided to take the towpath northbound; it was partially covered with mushy, melting snow, though the canal remained frozen over, but probably not thick enough to walk on. He gazed across the river valley at the town of Lehighton, which sprawled back up the hills to the west. Noise from the collective, morning activity of the town was just barely audible. Another runner passed headed in the opposite direction and exchanged hellos with Denny. He didn't know who he was. A dog was running with the guy too.

About a mile up the towpath, by a series of locks, Denny exited and took a winding steep hill that was a dirt access way up to Long Run Road. His legs had about turned to jelly by the time he crested the hill and got onto the back-country road, ironically named too, which he took for about a half of a mile downhill, before taking a side street that connected him to Fairyland Road, the main road that went through the heart of the township. Denny's hamstrings had indeed loosened up, and whatever was troubling his left calf had abated as well.

He thought about a conversation from years ago with his friend Bert in North Carolina about how nice it was to simply get out and run some days, for the pure sake of running. And Paul O'Connell, an old buddy he used to work with who had never run a race his entire life, and never desired to, yet faithfully woke up at four a.m. almost every morning to run. Denny wondered if he had done his annual 9-11 run last year, but then quickly realized it was a silly thought, since he already knew the answer. Gosh it would have been fourteen miles last September, as he would add one mile each year to mark the tragic date. Paul had been in the city then, a mere couple of miles from the twin towers.

For Denny today, it was one of those runs where the terrain and the time, and the subsequent miles, all sort of languidly rolled by. He stayed pleasantly lost with his own little sphere of thoughts; they came and went unobtrusively, keeping him company as he carried forth. As such, he had run up Indian Hill Road, and then had taken the right turn onto Walnut Street, crested one of its two big hills that bookended the road, and now had a clear view of the old baseball field he had played countless ballgames at as a kid.

It suddenly dawned on Denny that he was only a quarter of a mile or so from the house he had grown up in, a house he had not seen in over a decade. A bunch of blue jays were making a racket high up in the tree line that separated the grounds the baseball field was on, with the residential properties on the rest of the street. The sound of Denny's shoes hitting the macadam seemed to become more audible; he could now see the green sided, white bricked two-story house up ahead. He had travelled this road a thousand times, he had once known all the neighbors by name-

There was a black pickup truck in the driveway, and a small boat beside the house. A couple of the poplar trees which lined the perimeter of the side of the yard he was approaching had apparently been cut down, but for the most part all of it looked pretty much the same. Denny had no idea who was living there now; his sister had told him years ago that their father had sold the place and moved to Allentown to be closer to his new job. But that's about the extent of the details that he had been provided or had wanted.

As he ran by the front yard and looked over at the front of the house, Denny thought about the phone conversation that one fateful evening; for he had been in there, in the house, hadn't he? Yes, that much was an actual, unequivocal fact in the whole messy matter, whereas the rest of it all could be debated, interpreted, depending on one's point of view. Language could be parsed, words scrutinized, motives second guessed. But he had been there in that house alright, that was for certain; all Denny could seem to recall was the end of it, after all the yelling and recriminations. The final, parting words. Then, silence. By now, years' and years' worth of silence had accrued. Denny kept on running; the yard, the house, and all its memories remained behind, as he rounded another bend, and ran swiftly down the steep hill back towards Fairyland Road.

Denny headed back eastward into the rising sun, and into the rolling farm country he so dearly loved roaming around in on foot, or on a bicycle when growing up. Inside his head he heard a Pearl Jam song "Rearview Mirror"; I guess the beatings have made me wise he thought, and he wasn't about to apologize. Not today. Running into the sun felt warm and relaxing, almost cathartic at the moment, and he was glad he had decided to wear shorts. Denny wondered what Jennifer was up to. Nurturing the ill and tending to the weak. This thought nearly caused an audible outburst of laughter; over the years Denny had gradually become a little more able to recognize and accept his own faults, with enough of a modicum of levity to perhaps develop at least some of that precious commodity called humility. It was another thing to love about the roads and trails; the atmosphere was usually ripe for gut level honesty. Some days, a run could be like going to confession.

Back up in the apartment, Denny later went through his training log for the current year, and also fished out last year's log. He used the calculator function on his phone and began working on some tabulations, comparing the numbers from this year with those from the previous, which wasn't difficult to do, since the weekly, monthly, and yearly totals had already been written on the corresponding boxes and lines in the log books. Denny texted Trent the results." 2016: 7.59 mi/day. 54.15 mpw. Ahead of '15 pace by > 11 mpw. And he added "I'm just getting started my boy." Trent would appreciate; he was always doing his own calculations, a frequent topic of discussion of theirs. However, Trent used wall calendars to keep his tallies, and when they were running in school Denny always thought there was something intrinsically fascinating or super cool about the numbers scrawled in fine print inside the square boxes. Back then Denny used lined notebook pages to keep track of his runs, but it just didn't have the same cache.

And Denny felt like he was just getting started, not from a numerical frame of reference, but with the raison d'etre of the whole grandiose undertaking. He wanted to know if there were answers out there on the roads and trails, answers to questions he didn't even know how to ask. The mission was becoming a vital part of his lifeblood, transporting him beyond the normal strictures of daily living. Denny wasn't naïve, nor did he believe in a search for any kind of permanent escape from reality, but perhaps he could catch a glimpse behind the veil, and see the true indivisible nature of the world, and be able to translate his experiences into something utilitarian for himself and others. He had already had the light shine bright into his eyes; all of this now was house money he was playing with. So why not push his chips into the center of the table? A few minutes later Trent texted back with nothing but a big thumbs-up emoji, which did actually cause Denny to laugh aloud. I guess he's impressed he thought, as he tossed the phone onto the mattress.

Denny laid down on the mattress and set an alarm for 4:00pm just in case he drifted off to sleep, for plans had been made to go over to Jennifer's after she got off work, since her sons were with their father until after school Monday. As he laid there, looking again at the crack in the ceiling, his thoughts wandered back to his own father. Some of the earliest memories he had were about the fried egg sandwich stand they were proprietors of, and which was located conveniently at the bottom of their driveway, under the shade of a large maple tree. Customers could just pull up in their cars and order. The eggs were actually dippy eggs, or sunny side up as most others would refer to them, placed between two pieces of buttered toast. They were delicious too, though the whole stand thing out in the yard was of course fictional.

And there were all the days too when Denny would wake up early so he could tip toe down the hall and into the living room to sit on his Dad's lap as he read the newspaper before work. In the evening Denny, who couldn't have been more than three or four years old, would stand by the big bay windows and wait for him to come up the road and pull into the driveway. He probably would have been barely tall enough to even see out the windows.

Then of course there was all the running his Dad did, usually very early in the morning when it was still dark outside. He would run with Doug Hawkins, one of the neighbors a few houses up the street. They had established a system using outdoor lights to signal each other whether or not they were running. If the light was still on, so was the run. If it was off, no run. Or maybe it was the opposite? As Denny got older his Dad would sometimes come get him and take him on a shorter run with him, usually around what was referred to as the loop, a two-mile route which was a healthy challenge, since it contained numerous hills. On several occasions his Dad and running buddies trained for and ran marathons together. They would all pack into cars and head to the one guy's home in a nearby town, and while the men went out and hammered three-hour training runs, the wives and kids hung out in the house and found their own means of entertainment. Denny wondered if any of them still ran today. At some point too, he did drift off for a short nap.

Later Denny walked up to Jennifer's house via the same route traversed the day before. It was nice not to be so nervous, he thought as he walked by the cemetery. Jennifer answered the door in light blue hospital scrubs, and had her hair pulled back into two long pigtails. She was also wearing a pair of black rimmed glasses. "Golly jeez you look so cute," he whispered in her ear.

"Hush you."

"How was the hospital? Le hospitale."

"Lovely. No one died. At least not on my floor." Though she had told Denny shortly after they had first met up again that she loved being a nurse, which was also what her mother had done her whole career as well and had just retired from about a year and a half ago. Jennifer said it gave her a sense of purpose, especially at times when what a patient needed most was just someone to take care of them and show them that they in fact mattered. "They are people first, not just the sum of what diseases they have," she had written him one night when they were texting back and forth. Most of her patients were older and in the final stages of their twilight years.

"You hungry? I got Chinese from Yang Mings," Jennifer said over her shoulder, as Denny followed her in through the house and into the kitchen.

"Always." Yang's was a small restaurant on First Street that Denny had run by several times, but had never gone in, nor had gotten any food from before. But he would look inside as he passed the rows of windows; superficially to check out the two or three young Asian women working there, usually standing around over by a cashier's table behind which always stood a small, older woman with black hair pulled up in a bun and held together by what looked to be colored chopsticks. He wondered where they had come from, or more so, how they had ended up in this backwater, rural town in eastern Pennsylvania. And where did they live, what did they do, were they able to assimilate much, or did they even try to do so? Jennifer didn't have any particular information on the matter and was certainly not as intrigued about any of it either but could assure him from firsthand experience that the food was good.

She had picked up an order of sweet and sour pork, general Tso's chicken, and spicy pepper steak, with a container of pork fried race, and for good measure two egg rolls. "I was in the habit of going there once or twice a week this summer. Especially after football and soccer camp. They even knew my name."

"The Chinese girls?"

"I'm starting to think you have more than just a passing fancy with them."

Denny laughed. "It's all so damned fascinating to me."

"Times have changed buster. We've become much more cosmopolitan since you've been gone." Jennifer poured water into two glasses from a plastic pitcher and set one in front of him.

"I keep almost running the stop sign by the Legion. That was never there. And it took some time to adjust to the traffic light at the bottom of Ninth Street. You know I have a friend back in North Carolina who always asks questions like 'is there running water in Lehighton,' or 'is there a post office there', 'how about any pay phones?'"

"Lordy. Who is this son of a bitch?"

"Jim Aron. He's originally from Los Angeles."

"Well that explains it."

The food was good, especially the spicy pepper steak which had a gratifying, delayed heat to it. The jalapeno peppers mixed in kicked up the spice quotient as well, and Denny complimented Jennifer on another first-rate culinary decision. She herself looked content and pleased, as she dipped an egg roll into a plastic container of duck sauce. All of her little movements were a fount of small wonder to Denny

After they finished eating, Jennifer took Denny to the basement; the stairwell was accessed from a door in the dining room, and was dimly lit, while the boards of each step made a creaking noise as the two of them slowly descended into the cold, damp room. All of which added another layer of mystery to this apparently subterranean project that Jennifer had been passionately working on; she had offered Denny scant clues as to just what might be found below. Jennifer stopped suddenly on the last step, Denny almost fell into her and knocked her over.

"Easy champ."

"I'm okay."

"So..." she said with a more solemn intent, "please bear in mind that I have no formal training. And I just took this up a few years ago."

"I’m bearing in mind."

Jennifer grabbed Denny's hand and stepped down off the last step and led him a few more feet, then pulled a string that hung from the ceiling beneath a large bulb; the light revealed a room full of painted pictures, a few of which were on easels, and many more that were scattered about the floor and propped up against the walls, or in front of boxes and crates, with one larger painting sitting atop a wooden rocking chair.

"Wow," was about the extent that Denny could verbally muster, as he took it all in. The explosion of colors is what immediately caught his eyes. Reds, yellows, oranges swirled onto black backgrounds, in all sorts of patterns, shapes. Blues and greens, like tropical waters, made floating pyramids, or diamonds extending out of concentric circles, contrasted with bright white or charcoal grey colors. Denny slowly, as if transfixed, moved amongst the paintings, careful not to come too close, like he was walking into a shop full of fine china.

"This is all so amazing!" he finally exclaimed.

Jennifer stood off to the side by the water heater, with her hands inside of her pants pockets. "Thank you," she softly replied, in stark contrast to the volume her artwork spoke.

"I'm not an art critic but they are all so striking. I had no idea you painted."

Jennifer unfolded a lawn chair and sat down. Denny instinctively flipped over an empty bucket and sat down on top of it, next to a pile of paints and newspapers lying on the cement floor.

"It's my very own underground studio. Literally."

"I love it. This is so awesome. When did you get into all of this? There must be hundreds of paintings in here." Denny was blown away by the pure visuals of it, though he knew little about artwork or painting. He always thought that artist's studios looked so cool, not that he had ever really been in any, but likely had seen pictures over the years that helped form his opinion of such. And this was most definitely cool, down here in this basement. Almost secretive, taboo, wild and evocative. Plus, it was like stepping into the interior of another person's being, catching a peek at their soul.

"I've been painting for about four years now. There's a bunch of stuff at my mom's house too. And I like to give them away as little gifts or thank-yous. Some of my patients take them home with them from the hospital and hang them up. Or so they've told me."

Denny rocked a little back and forth on the bucket. Jennifer continued, "it just depends on what I think they represent. Each painting that is. Or how I was feeling when I was painting it. I don't know, I just do what feels right."

"I understand."

"Oh?"

"Actually, I don't. My apologies I'm not an artist."

"You're a writer Den."

Denny didn't respond as he stood up and went over to look closer at some of the individual paintings lined up against the far wall. "Some of these..." she stopped, as Denny bent over to look at a particular canvas which appeared to be some sort of disfigured dark reddish face tangled in a black spider like web and looked to him like something off of a Pink Floyd album cover.

"Some bad shit happened," he could hear Jennifer say from behind him. The grave seriousness of her voice was unmistakable, so Denny walked back over and sat down on the bucket again. He thought about something he had read about Buddhism and the alleviation of suffering, but he didn't say anything as he wasn't too sure he understood much of it anyway. This didn't seem like a good moment to be fundamentally wrong about something, even if it was in the spirit of trying to be helpful. And the moment was hers, not his anyway.

"Well," she smiled, while wiping away a tear from her eyes, "I didn't see it at first. Or I pretended not to. I guess it's so hard to swallow some things that denial becomes really therapeutic. In the short term. I don't know. I guess it’s one of those things like you see in the movies or hear about it happening to someone else. But it's never you. Right?"

Denny leaned forward on the bucket; it almost tipped over, but he caught himself up just in time.

"After a while you go numb to it, or it becomes a part of you. The secret part you hide from the world, even to those who are closest to you. But they know. They know sooner or later." Jennifer raised the tenor of her voice the last sentence. "Which made it all so embarrassing then as well. I felt a lot of shame. Plus, I'm a nurse. Crazy right?"

"Right."

"Anyhow I had a hard time looking my sons in the eyes for a while. I mean they were younger then but Jake was getting old enough to start figuring things out. And my mom didn't even want to come by the house anymore. Wow sometimes I wished I still smoked." She managed a little laugh.

"I'd offer you a light."

"Denny, he abused the shit out of me. Physically at times too. One night he even pulled a gun on me when the kids were upstairs in our old house sleeping. Put it right up against my temple. Kept yelling 'how does it feel how does it feel?'"

"Jesus."

"But you know that's when I had my moment of clarity like you guys talk about. That's when I decided I was done with all of it. If he didn't kill me right then and there it was too bad for him. Because I was going to start over in life without him."

"I had no idea Jennifer."

"Well it's not something you share with the whole world," she said with a little more of a laugh this time. "At least I wouldn't. So anyhow that is about when I started painting. Or soon after. That one with the face you were looking at over there is one of the first ones I made. While I was waiting for the divorce to go through."

"It's quite powerful."

"Thank you," Jennifer replied as she wiped aside a few more tears from her face. "I assure you I'm not really the mess you may think I am."

"Well even if you were..." She threw a paint brush at him.

"How can you miss from five feet away?"

"You." Jennifer looked on the ground presumably for something else to chuck but Denny was too quick for her as he bounded up off the bucket, went over and grabbed both of her arms and started to lift her out of the chair, all in one fell swoop.

"Come here. You." Denny held her tight and could hear her faintly sobbing on his shoulder.

"I'm ok," she said after a few moments, then took him around her studio and talked about some of the different works of art she had created. There was an effervescent energy bubbling forth from her every movement, an almost hypnotic frenzy in the way she supplied details and background to the various paintings. "Some days I can't wait to get home and get down here." Jennifer picked up one particular painting off the ground, it looked like some kind of spinning wheel of rainbow like bright colors flaming across the canvas. "I painted this the night after I saw you in the school," she said as she handed him the picture. "I want you to have it."

"Thank you. I'm touched."

"From the sounds of it you could use a little something to hang up on the walls over there." She smiled as she punched Denny lightly in the arm.

"I love it."

Chapter 6

Working remotely was going alright, and Denny got some days off between projects which he spent doing a lot of reading. He read a book by a runner named Travis Macy called *The Ultra Mindset,* and finished a collection of Thomas Merton's writings, before beginning a book about Saint Francis de Sales. His friend Jerry also dropped him off *The Da Vinci Code* which he had never read, or to Jennifer's incredulity, had never seen the movie either. He also did some writing as well, posting some rambling thoughts on a blog he had started years ago but never kept up, and jotted down some more notes in his trusted notebook. Denny also re-read several sections in his Jack Daniel's book. One morning he helped Keith install a sink and cabinets in one of the downstairs units that some tenants were about to move in to, though he doubted he was much help. He kind of figured too that his friend mostly wanted someone to talk to.

And of course, he ran. One afternoon Denny headed down to First Street, but instead of taking the Weissport Bridge across the river, he decided to get across by using the trestle. To access, required him to run on a rut filled narrow dirt road, to use the term loosely, which began behind Dunbar's warehouse, and was primarily used by busses and other vehicles to pick up white water rafters and tubers who would disembark on an open, yet rocky section of clearing beside the river. How those busses got thru amazed Denny, since their windows must be constantly rubbing up against shrubs and tree branches, if the bus itself didn't get stuck in the mud in the first place.

Denny didn't have to worry about any of that traffic in the wintertime; he found a steep little pathway that led through the trees to the railroad tracks, about twenty meters up from the trestle, which had been rebuilt since Denny had last run across it back in the less cautious days of his youth. The rickety boards parallel to the tracks had been replaced with metal grating, which afforded views of the rushing waters maybe a hundred feet below. He ignored the 'No Trespassing. Property of the Norfolk Railroad,' sign and headed across, not before checking the track behind him for trains, though in all his numerous trips across in the past none had ever come while he was actually on the trestle.

On the opposite side of the river, Denny took a short dirt trail that connected to the towpath. He had decided on the fly to tweak the workout listed in the Daniel's plan, a thirty-minute threshold run, and instead do a hard out and back up to the observation deck, about two and half miles to the north. Plus, he was in the mood for a little fun, and sought to establish a FKT, or fastest known time, on the towpath. Whether or not one actually existed he did not know, nor was that detail terribly important, as Denny set out at a good clip in the mid to high six-minute per mile range, with the plan of slowly, but steadily, increasing the tempo, thus turning it into a progression run. He always liked the phrase "turning the screw" used to describe when a runner methodically, but almost imperceptibly increased their pace in order to wear down, and eventually drop the competition. Denny's only competition today would be himself, and of course all those other make-believe runners who had posted times on the course previous to today's run. God, he did love the simplicity of the sport.

Denny felt good, and just sort of let the run develop and flow, like the waters of the Lehigh River he could see in his peripheral vision through the bare trees, on what seemed like such a tranquil, sunny, weekday afternoon. The ice atop the canal was broken up in parts; some pools of water laid exposed, though it was too early to be thinking about spring time. Denny recalled many track practices in March running around huge snow piles in the school parking lots or running indoors around the auditorium when it was too cold and windy to be outdoors. Somebody fell real hard one time in there; they tripped over a raised part of the stage where the lights popped up out of, but he couldn't remember who it was. It was damned funny though. The watch beeped and read 6:38 for the first mile.

His thoughts seemed to drift along with his body, as he had been getting lost for a bit in a most positive and enjoyable way in many of the words he had been reading. Denny pictured some of the countryside in Kentucky that Merton was so fond of and imagined he would have liked the outdoors here as well. The lush rolling hills in the summer time, juxtaposed with the tranquil, less colorful beauty of the winter months. Before he knew it, his watch beeped again, and read 6:26 for mile number two. And shortly thereafter he was climbing the wooden steps of the observation tower, which wasn't a tower, but more like an open-air deck, with a magnificent view of the river and surrounding valley. Denny made note as he climbed down, that the steps must be included as part of the FKT.

His breathing was steady, controlled. His strides fluid; he would occasionally repeat to himself "just cover ground," a phrase he was inclined to say to his runners when engaged in a tougher workout. Track and field would be starting down there in under two weeks, but Denny had told Shane the head coach and good friend of his, that he wouldn't be there until likely later in the season, though truthfully, he wasn't sure; it was one of the unfortunate, negative conditions of his northward sojourn. But he was trying not to think much at all about any of that, and to just trust the process, and to trust that he was supposed to be where he was supposed to be and would eventually go where he was supposed to go. Blind faith perhaps? He hit the three-mile mark in 6:19 and followed that up with a 6:12 mile. Denny was moving along pretty dam good.

He passed the set of locks by the Long Run Road entrance, then started the long sweeping bend where the canal and river are separated by a dense section of woods. Denny knew this stretch of real estate so very well and could mete out his efforts in accordance to where he knew he was, in relation to what he had left to go. Once he cleared the bend and crossed a small elevated foot bridge, there was less than a half mile left to go. By now he was running about as fast as he could, while still trying to stay in control, something that the best runners could almost make look effortless in their economies of motion. Denny glanced over at the trestle as he flew by the open space; he equated that there was less than four-hundred meters on a track left to be run, and he told himself again "cover ground, cover ground." And he did cover ground, rather fast; he broke the tape at the pretend finish line moments after he had gone through the fifth mile in 5:53. Denny hit his chest with a fist then pointed skyward and gave thanks; he gasped for air while slowly meandering into the gravel parking lot, looking himself a bit punch drunk, but pleased as punch with his overall time of 31:36. With that, a new FKT on the towpath had been set. "Time to party," he wheezed to all the Canadian geese gathered by the edge of the canal. A few of them honked in approval.

One seemingly innocuous night, long after Denny had returned from sneaking into see Jennifer at her house after her kids had gone to sleep, the ringing of his cell phone awoke him. There have only been a few specific times in his life when he knew before answering a phone call, that some sort of bad news was awaiting him on the other end of the line. It's an eerie feeling, which does not lend itself to a rational explanation; the last time was when his aunt called to tell him that his mother had died. Tonight, it was Suzanne's voice on the phone.

"Denny are you awake?"

"Yes. What is it?"

"Keith. We are at the hospital."

"What?"

"He's alright. Stable."

"What's going on?"

"I guess he tried to take his life. Not sure. There was a note."

"Jesus. Is he okay?"

"Yes. Well he's not ok. But he's alive and stable. I'm sorry I shouldn't have called so late." It sounded like she had been crying, and her voice seemed far off.

"I'll be right there let me get dressed."

"No don't. There's nothing to do tonight. He's sedated." She paused for several seconds. The silence on the phone was intense. "He'll be in here for a while though."

"Okay. I'm so sorry." Denny was scrambling for something more to say, though what did come out was probably the best thing that could. "I'm praying for you guys," he said.

"Thanks. I'm going to go now."

"Good night Sue." Denny tossed the phone beside him on the mattress, and stared ahead at one of the walls, at the painting he had hung from Jennifer; its outline was just barely visible. He briefly thought about calling her but decided against it. The room was filled with such a deafening silence, as Denny strained to hear any kind of noise, perhaps as a way to try and comprehend if what had just happened was in fact real. But he knew it was; he laid back down and closed his eyes and pictured Keith, and pictured his face with a smile on it, perhaps the purest form of prayer there was. He thought of the family too, and pictured each one of them as well, while adding may the angels of mercy be by your sides.

Denny awoke early the next morning, shortly after daybreak; for a few moments the events of last night were unclear, but as he made his way into the cold kitchen to make coffee he knew it was real, and not some bad dream. He looked out the window and thought about where to run; for he knew without knowing, that it was the glue that kept his own life together. As he took the warm cup into his hands, steam rising off the surface, Denny did know too that there were no guarantees in any of this.

The air outside was also cold, but that sort of pure clean cold that is refreshing. There was little wind blowing and the sun was out, illuminating an almost cloudless blue sky. Denny decided to dedicate the run to Keith, and to take one his favorite routes up into the heights and past the Ukrainian Homestead, which he figured his friend would enjoy. As he glanced sideways at the rising sun which was about to crest the hills to the east, Denny thought about some lines of Jim Morrison's poetry, "give us an hour to perform our art, and to perfect our lives."

A couple of evenings later, after Denny had finished his dinner of a burrito filled with brown rice and black beans, and a baked sweet potato, he got into his car and drove out to the hospital to visit Keith. He was on the top floor, the seventh floor, which was off-handedly known by all to be the mental ward. When Denny arrived at the correct room, he found Keith sitting up in bed and watching television, while Ron and Nicole were sitting on chairs over by the window. Nicole was playing some kind of hand held video game and didn't even look up as Denny walked through the room. Suzanne was still down the hallway talking to one of the doctors.

"Looks like I'm not too late for the party, though I left the vegetable tray in the car." When confronted with uncomfortable situations, Denny's means of coping was to fall back upon humor, though he realized after he spoke how asinine he sounded.

"It's okay, they don't eat them anyway," Keith said from the bed, while not taking his eyes off the mounted television set attached to the front wall. The gravity of the situation bore down on Denny quickly; he stood off to the side of the bed, which had metal railings that extended about a foot and a half above the mattress. An IV was stuck in Keith's one arm, and an array of machines churned out medical data, which lit up on various small monitors placed just off the front side of the bed. His heart rate was 64, that much could be comprehended by Denny, who also thought that wasn't too bad for someone who hadn't run much of late. Though he didn't know what kind of medication was being administered.

"Sit down or something," Keith instructed, apparently aware of the observations being made. "Ron get off the chair and take Nic to the cafeteria or something."

"It's closed now," Ron responded, while also focused on the television set.

"Suzanne is coming back soon to get them," Keith said, presumably to Denny. He looked a bit haggard and pale lying in bed, but other than that he kind of seemed the same as he did when Denny saw him a few days ago.

"It's alright. I just popped in for a few minutes," Denny said as he walked across the room. "Whatcha playing?" he asked Nicole.

"Gemini adventures," she answered into the game.

Denny looked out the window and across the parking lot way down below, and into the dark hills and woods of Mahoning Township which disappeared westward into the night. He had never been up on the seventh floor; must be a nice view during the daytime he thought. Denny strained his eyes as he continued to look out the window and into the night, as if he was expecting something to appear to him from beyond his field of vision.

"Hey guys," Suzanne said as she entered the room, and then gave Denny a smile as he turned around. She walked over and stood by Keith's bedside. God what she must be going through as well, and the kids too, which he hadn't really thought much about, instead more focused with what was up with Keith and just what exactly he had done to land up in here. How depressed, or angry, or whatever he must have been, though he suspected it may just have been some kind of loud cry for help, and thankfully nothing permanent and more calamitous had occurred.

Denny felt a touch guilty standing there, realizing just how selfish and self-absorbed he could be at times, as a quick mental review could easily identify numerous times that his friend had been attempting to reach out. Though in Denny's defense, he had been there and listened, and wasn't sure what more could have been done. The sound of Final Jeopardy roused Denny from his mental tangent; so, this is what it's like to be in the madhouse popped into Denny's head, as he walked over and gave Suzanne a long hug,

"Easy she's still legally my wife." Keith said rather matter of fact. A nurse walked in and said good evening, then proceeded to check the monitors as well as the drip of the IV bag, which hung from a contraption similar to a squared off shepherd's crow. She made some notes inside of a hard-plastic clipboard, then quickly walked back out the door. Denny wondered if she knew Jennifer.

"Let's go guys you have school tomorrow."

"I'm not finished," protested Nicole.

"Shut down the game and listen to your Mom," said Keith, with just enough forceful irritation in his voice to compel his daughter to immediately comply. Once they left, he picked up the remote control from the bed stand and started changing the channels, one at a time. "Has to be a basketball game on," he sort-of half muttered. Denny sat down on one of the chairs and looked out the window again, below he could see some people walking together through the parking lot. They all got inside the same car, which drove out of the lot.

Denny looked over at Keith. "Sorry amigo, was just watching people down in the lot."

"It's fine."

"I just wanted to stop by and say hey. And let you know if there is anything I can do or anything I can help out with to..."

"I know." Keith interrupted. He had found a college basketball game on and had set the remote back down on the bed stand. They both sat there and watched the game for a few minutes, not saying anything. Denny flashed back to the NCAA bracket pools that Keith used to organize and run many years ago. The tourney would be starting next week, and Denny wondered if perhaps Keith was thinking the same thing too. It all suddenly seemed like a million miles away inside that room tonight. When Denny glanced over at Keith again on the bed his eyes were closed. He stood up and quietly walked over to the end of the bed and saw that his friend was asleep.

Denny saw the nurse who had come into the room in the hallway and told her that Keith was asleep. That's not surprising she said, since he was on some heavier medication. Denny wondered what kind of medication, but didn't ask; instead he said goodnight, and caught the elevator back to the lobby. As Denny strode through the parking lot he looked up at the row of windows on the top floor; it's a fine line sometimes, a fine line indeed.

Chapter 7

Winter was about to draw to a conclusion, at least as defined by the calendar. And the weather seemed to have fallen in lock step, as high temperatures soared into the fifties for several straight days. Shorts had become the common attire on runs, accompanied up top by perhaps only so much as a long sleeve Tec shirt many an early evening, one of which Denny met Trent at the D&L trailhead. It was a balmy fifty-one degrees at 5:30pm, as the two of them set off southward.

"Man, this is nice," Trent stated, as they settled into a brisker running pace; an older, fit looking woman passed by running rather smoothly, back towards the parking lot. Everyone exchanged pleasantries.

"I think she was at the race the other week."

"Probably. I've seen her a bunch down here."

"She sat on me through two and a half miles, but I surprised her by starting my kick from eight-hundred meters out and dropping her."

"Gets them every time."

"Think she won the sixty and over age group."

"Probably would have beaten me," Trent added. The two runners made their way down into one of the more secluded, wooded stretches, where there were still some patches of snow well up on the steep slope of the Mahoning Mountain, but for the most part any traces of winter had all but vanished. "Damn it's good to be running outdoors again."

"I'll bet."

"Let's do six miles."

"Sure thing pops."

The ground was damp and mushy soft as they rolled down towards Bowmanstown, a sleepy little village of about a thousand people, and the childhood home of Denny's mother. Two women rode by on bikes, the wheels of which made a faint squishy noise until it faded out of earshot. Trent asked, "you been seeing Jennifer a lot?"

"Yeah. For the most part. Been a nice couple of weeks."

"I always thought she was cool." He paused for a few seconds, as they matched strides. "Plus, her oldest son is a good wrestler."

"He's 15 and 6 now. Fifth seed going into regionals."

"Nice. Cody is seeded second at one twelve."

Denny checked his watch; the two old teammates were currently running a 7:20 per mile pace. Up ahead they could see route 895, the road which bisected Bowmanstown on either side of the river, then headed west, parallel to the base of the Blue Mountain. The turnaround point, or three-mile mark, was just before the road. Denny felt good, and so did Trent presumably; he wasn't breathing too audibly. After turning around, Trent said with a wisp of devilish mien, "maybe you'll stick around and become a wrestling step dad like me."

"It's always been an ambition of mine. Since I excelled so much at the sport in gym class." Denny had hated the annual few weeks in the winter that they had to wrestle. Back then he had very little upper body strength and wasn't much of what one would call a fighter.

"I can teach you some stuff."

"Thanks, my man. Actually, I have no idea what I am doing with Jennifer. But it's super fun right now. It's like we leaped right back in to where we were all those years ago. Kinda crazy right?"

Trent didn't answer, perhaps sensing that the question was best left dangling in a rhetorical fashion, or he was just wise enough not to proffer any romantic advice. Denny could feel himself slowly stepping on the accelerator and increasing the pace, his means of diverting subjects which he wasn't fully comfortable with; in this case a matter of the heart that he knew was much more textually layered than perhaps he was looking for while up here. But he caught the folly in his logic, since it ran counter to his philosophy of what runs encompass, in that out here any and all subjects were brought to bear, without discrimination. And what happened out here conversationally, stayed out here. Plus, Trent was hanging right with him, and didn't seemed fazed by the uptick in the tempo, and was in better shape than Denny, or Trent himself thought. The sun's light was fading fast; it was peacefully serene running through the twilight alongside the river.

"I don't know what I am going to do," Denny let out, almost involuntarily. "This whole thing really took me by surprise. Though I do believe in second chances. What are the odds though? But I had told myself at the very longest I'd stay here six months." The two runners ran for a bit in silence, their strides in unison again. "I'm missing track season down there. I'm the long-distance coach, but we have two others who can fill in. But I won't miss Cross Country in the fall. Be my third year as head coach. I'm just conflicted. And I haven't figured out how to be in two places at once."

Trent didn't say too much in response; but he understood his buddy's quandary and wished he had some answers that could help him out. He did tell him that he couldn't imagine life without Jill, no matter where he was. Denny realized too that Trent was probably hoping that he'd consider moving back up permanently, as perhaps Keith did, and maybe Jennifer now. There were reasons why Denny felt like he could never do that, but they were reasons he was not going to talk to Trent about, at least in not any direct fashion, for he hated to think that any of his friends would ever perceive that he was looking down upon living there. And for many of them, like Trent, it was a good choice; they had built contended, purposeful lives here. But for Denny, he had travelled a different road, which he felt was one of the best decisions he had ever made in his life. Yet here he was back on his old home turf, churning out seven-minute miles with his oldest running pal.

Back at the trailhead's parking lot Trent and Denny hung out for a few minutes and chatted away; they had completed the six-mile run in 44:26. Trent was stoked about the effort and beaming with pride, as he thanked Denny for the hard work out. "It's really good to have you around," he said while getting into his car, "even if it is for just awhile."

Denny waved as he pulled out onto the street and said, "thank you," into the placid sky.

He sat down in the back of the Rav4 and looked on down the D&L Trail that him and Trent had just run. The sun had fallen below the hills to the west, and darkness had just about blanketed the area, which brought a drop in temperature. Denny felt a bit nippy; he donned his heavy University of North Carolina-Wilmington sweatshirt, and also his black Eagles beanie and a pair of gloves, as he had decided to go for an impromptu cool down walk through the lower part of town.

He headed up past the old Woolworth's store, and down First Street to the Carbon Mini Mart, which forever lived in Denny's mind as the 7-11 that it used to be twenty, thirty years ago. There was still a Slurpee machine there, plus ones containing coffee out of which he filled a twelve-ounce cup, while also purchasing a copy of the local afternoon newspaper, *The Times News.* On the front page there was an article about a drug sting in the town of Tamaqua; four dealers had been arrested after a six-month undercover operation coordinated by the FBI.

Jerry was worried that his daughter might be doing heroin, which surprised Denny, until he was told just how pervasive the drug had become in the area, along with narcotics such as Oxycodone and Percocet, which was a far cry from the drug scene when he last lived here. Back then it was marijuana, and if you had a good connection, cocaine. But even that was kept pretty secretive; anything harder than pot that is. Nowadays it was practically out in the open, all of it. When Denny ran through certain sections of town it was as if an invisible cloud hung over ahead; the socio-economic conditions which seemed to spawn the epidemic were almost tangible. He was told too that in the small towns to the north, up in the "coal cracking" region the problems were even worse. Two young teenage girls walked past Denny, one of them smiled and said, "hey man." He kept on walking.

This wasn't his home anymore; he knew it, as he walked past the old folks hi-rise building and headed back down to where his car was parked. Denny knew that he couldn't stay here permanently, for it would be like going backwards. On some level he was trying to recapture a little something from the past that was long since gone, which he was beginning to see was best to recall from a certain distance and perspective only achievable when physically not present. Though it was nice to tap into these mostly idyllic memories for short bursts of time, but similar to circling laps on his old track, if he hung around too long they lost their freshness and could turn bitter and stale. Or it all just became a little too heartbreaking; as much as we sometimes may desire to do so, we simply cannot go back in time. But when he was lying there with Jennifer, or running with Trent-

Early the next morning, as Denny was running in the heights along one of the ridgelines, he caught sight of the valley; some of the fog which had settled in overnight had begun to dissipate, and he realized once again how fortunate he was to be in his own little running paradise, and how he wouldn't trade this off right here for just about anything. I'm so damned lucky he thought, to have all of this; miles upon miles of challenging running terrain in some of the most stunning scenery, in a place I know so well. And to top it off, there are friends here who run and love running in their own personal ways like I do.

He was like a surfer chasing the waves; Denny had discovered that some of the best highs could be attained in this vast extension of his old backyard. Happiness was in Denny's heart; he was perhaps gaining a better understanding of the dichotomies he had been feeling the past two, three months, or at least it didn't vex him as much as he caromed down off the steep hill past the Orioles Club and descended into the thick woods of the valley below. A fast-moving stream kept him company as he wound past the convalescent home where his grandmother had spent the last few years of her life. Denny said a prayer for her, and his grandfather, as he made his way out of the forest and out onto route 902, which would take him back into town.

Denny drove back over one evening to the hospital to see Keith. Jennifer accompanied him as well; they had dinner beforehand at the Boulevard Restaurant, which Denny loved for its big salad bar, which was also to his knowledge the only salad bar in town. He had broiled mountain trout with a baked potato and steamed asparagus, to go along with his salad, while Jennifer had the beef stroganoff. She let Denny try some off her plate; the norm when they ate out together, though Jennifer would usually say no to his reciprocal offer. He hadn't tasted beef stroganoff most likely since he and his sister would go with their mom to visit one of her old college friends in Pottsville, about an hour or so drive away. Joyce was her name, and apparently, she liked to make the meal often, or at least when they came to visit her at her house, which was actually a converted trailer. Denny had forgotten what the name of the dish was called and hadn't thought about Joyce since speaking with her at his Mom's funeral.

When they got to the hospital, Jennifer went to go work-out in the employee gym. She even planned to incorporate some running into her evening routine. "I won't run on the roads yet in public but I'll use the treadmill. I'm a work in progress," she said as she stood holding the door to go inside.

"I'm proud of you my tough little warrior princess."

"Yeaaahh right."

"See you in a bit."

"Send Keith my regards." With that she entered the gym on the first floor, and Denny walked back over to the lobby to take the elevator to the infamous seventh floor. When he got to the room, Keith was sitting up in his bed reading a magazine, the television was on in the background.

"Come in," he said

"Hola amigo. Como estas?"

"Wacked from all the drugs. Hell, I don't even know half of what they are putting in me."

Denny walked over and grabbed one of the chairs and spun it around by the window to face Keith. "You look better. They feeding you alright?"

"Food is the least of my worries," he responded. Then added, "I guess so."

Denny clapped his hands once in front of himself and looked down at the floor. Pent up curiosity could no longer be contained. "So, just what the heck happened?" he asked.

Keith adjusted his body on the bed, grabbed another pillow and placed it behind his back, then set the magazine down on the bed stand. After what seemed like an interminable amount of time he finally spoke. "Well I'm not sure on some of it, but I had started drinking that day well before dinner. But later I took a bunch of these pills I have for anxiety, especially at work, and apparently at some point I wrote a note and left it on the kitchen counter not to bother me. That I was going to sleep for a very long time. I don't even remember writing it. But Suzanne showed it to me later. In fact, I don't recall much except feeling like this giant invisible weight was bearing down on my chest and was finally about to crush me for good. I didn't think I could breathe. Or felt like I couldn't. Was about to be suffocated, and that's a horrible way to go. I guess I wanted some sort of resolution." Keith adjusted the pillows again behind him and looked ahead at the television set.

"Guess God had other plans."

"There you go again with religion." He didn't look over at Denny when he made the remark, instead his eyes stayed fixed on the television, which Denny decided to do himself as well. A MASH episode was on; he had seen this one before. Some halfwit North Korean flying a wobbly propeller plane kept trying to drop a bomb on the unit. But every time it ended up way off target and up in the surrounding hills.

Finally, Denny asked again, "is there anything I can do for you?"

"I don't think so. But thanks."

Denny though felt like he needed to do or say something. Perhaps that would give his friend some glimmer of hope, a life preserver if you will. But that didn't really make sense did it? That's what the hospital was for right? Denny had also learned that sometimes people cannot be helped, no matter what our intentions may be for them. But that would not deter him, so he began, "look I know all the particulars are not the same. And of course, I cannot fully grasp what you are going through personally." Denny leaned forward a little and clapped his hands together one time again. "But like I've said before, the running was always something I could come back to or turn to. Even when I wasn't sure of why. Maybe it just gives me a little precious time away from whatever troubles I may be facing. Or like I remember my Dad used to say that if he ran, no matter what else happened in the day, he had accomplished one positive thing."

Keith looked over at him and replied rather curtly, "running isn't the damned answer to everything. Quit being so childish."

The words kind of stung Denny a bit, and surprised him to say the least, though he had to concede that there could be some validity to what Keith had said. Yes, perhaps it was sort of foolish and simplistic to suggest that by simply going for a run, life's problems would somehow begin to melt on away. But Denny was not ready to retreat just yet from the foundations of such a philosophy; he had too much first-hand data to believe otherwise.

Stripping things back to the barer essentials had allowed him to continue to peer deeper into not only his own life, but the collective life force both visible and invisible around him. Though he was hard pressed to articulate much more than the surface observations; his poverty was far from complete, and he was honest enough to realize it never would be.

So, he replied, "yeah I know Keith. I'm just glad that you are okay." Radar was on the intercom calling attention to the comical little fighter pilot, who was again inbound for their camp. And once again the plane coughed and sputtered, before dropping its meager payload well up into the hills again, and out of harm's way.

"I'm not okay," Keith then did respond. He picked up the remote and started flipping through the channels. "But thanks though."

Denny took leave a little later and went for a walk around the hospital grounds, then came back in to find Jennifer. She was sitting sort of hunched over on a bench in the lobby. Sweat was streaming down the sides of her face, as she took a drink from a plastic bottle.

"Hey superstar."

She looked up with an almost wild, bug eyed look on her face. "Don't hey superstar me! Why the hell didn't you warn me not to run after eating like that? I almost puked in a trash can next to some guy riding a bike. He's one of the doctors on the Board too."

"Oh my."

"Oh my is right!" She did manage to laugh a little, albeit somewhat maniacally. She did look rather distressed. "I ought to punch you in the head. But I'm too weak. Take me home buster."

"I didn't think you were going to try that much of a run. My apologies." Denny should have known better. Underestimating Jennifer always proved to be a grievous mistake.

"Yeah, yeah, yeah."

When they got into the parking lot, and away from the main entrance, Denny stopped and grabbed ahold of her and gave her a big hug, holding Jennifer as tight as he could, as if he could pull her whole body into his.

"Oohhhh," she said softly.

Back home in the apartment he thought some more about Keith's response to running. Denny knew that it all couldn't just be some kind of vehicle to drive away and hide from the vagaries of life itself; though at times out on the roads, the diversions from the more mundane trivialities was welcomed, and certainly sought after. It was a good place to burn off all the accumulated crap, and a good way to burn off all that undefinable somberness and negativity that was apt to roam around inside of a lot of us, especially Denny at times.

He thought about Mylene, a girl in high school he had coached for several years. One time while out on a run, she had told him that since she had started running, she felt like she had become a better person, and was deeply appreciative that the sport had found her. Maybe it was as simple as that? As he walked over and peered out the side window into the darkness, he had far more questions than answers, which led him to believe that he was right where he wanted to be and needed to be.

Denny had run sixty-four miles last week, his best week of the year. Overall, he was running about as much as he ever had in his life, when also factoring in the intensity of the Jack Daniel's workouts performed a couple times per week. And he continued to stay after his ancillary work and found a certain discipline in the daily toil; thriving on each new challenge to see how much could be tolerated. He knew there had to be breaking points, right? Denny wanted to find them, and smash through them. And the physical aspect of it but was one part of the whole, when it came to encountering new boundaries, and ascertaining what may lie beyond. He was an experiment of one, something he had read years ago in a George Sheehan book. Like a scientist tinkering about in their lab, or an engineer tooling about in their garage, Denny was a part of this vanguard; on the front lines in search of new discoveries, not only in the temporal world of formulas and equations, but in the boundless spiritual universe as well. His "AHA" moments came on the open roads, where he was unconstrained, able to practice his religion in one colossal, far reaching temple; the sacraments were the sound of his shoes hitting the ground.

And he was trying to stay diligent with his writing as well, though it was the weakest link in the chain being assembled. Denny liked to talk to Jennifer often about her painting, not only because he had fallen back in love with her, but the characteristics of what she did with brush in hand helped him to develop his own approaches to the written word. She had told him that she liked to paint when the spirit moved her, when something was bubbling up inside and just had to come out. If she tried to work on some sort of set schedule the results would be dull and uninspiring. Certainly not with the creative flair she liked her paintings to exude. And once those creative juices began to flow, Jennifer might stay up half the night down in her studio. One time, she told him with a laugh, she even forgot to pick up the boys after wrestling practice. "Thank God they didn't tell their Dad," she added.

Some nights Denny would bundle up and go sit outside in the little backyard behind the house and attempt to meditate by sitting cross legged on the ground. When there was snow cover, he took an old towel to sit on. With eyes closed, Denny would try and stop his mind from having any thoughts, or when any thoughts did come, he would try and let them roll away, and instead focus on his breathing, in and out, in and out. Or he would just use such feeble, yet genuine attempts at meditation, more so as prayer sessions, by again visualizing the person's face with a smile, as he sent positive thoughts and energy to them, while asking God to watch over all.

And Denny felt too that it really didn't matter what others may think about his peculiar eccentricities, or how he was choosing to spend his time and own energy. For he truly believed that someday some good would be born out of all this. I can't be the only one who has felt like this or feels like I do at times he reasoned. I'm not that different; I'm not the only person who doesn't want to subscribe to what would be considered the normal conventions as defined by society writ large. There are many more outliers like me, pursing their own crazy little adventures and dreams. When Denny listened closely, their drumbeats echoed off the mountains, and on down through the valleys. They all beat time with sticks softer than a bird's feathers. Many, had had their faces pushed to the ground long enough; the taste of freedom was very sweet indeed.

Chapter 8

Denny decided to go to the new high school track one evening for his workout. The new all-weather surface had almost a sponge like springiness. I could lay a baby down on this Denny thought, as he set his backpack down on the infield grass. A younger girl ran by; she looked like she was probably an underclassman in high school. He slipped off his track pants and pulled out from his bag a new pair of Saucony Kinetta Relays, which had just arrived via the mail a few days ago. They were his third pair; he loved doing harder runs while wearing, though the tread did seem to wear out pretty fast. But the price was rather inexpensive, especially for running shoes. He kept on a heavier long-sleeved t-shirt, beanie and gloves as he stepped onto the track to first run an easy twenty-minute warm-up.

A man, perhaps the girl's father, or coach, stood off down by the one end zone. Denny amused himself, wondering if they knew he was the former school record holder in the 1600 meters. Two older ladies also arrived, and started slowly jogging in the outside lanes, just as he had completed his warm-up.

On the menu for Denny D. was a set of twelve times 200 meters, at repetition pace, with an equal distance recovery jog. Or rolling 200s as he liked to refer to them as at track practices. Thirty-eight seconds was the target time; per the numbers found in one of the Jack Daniel's book's charts and derived from his last five-kilometer race time, minus some allotted adjustment for the snow on part of the course. After the warm up-run, Denny slowly walked up to the appropriate track markings where he'd commence the 200s, then turned to look behind him at the Mahoning Mountain, visible beyond the far end zone, and above the high, open metal fencing. Everything always looked so calm right before one is to hurtle themselves into the breach. Denny had struggled during his last workout, a set of three, ten-minute threshold runs, with only two minutes recovery time. But it had been windy out, and he had also been concerned about some emails from work about scheduling changes.

He took off his long sleeve shirt, though it was pretty cold out, with temperatures falling through the thirties by now. He kept his gloves and beanie on, and took a couple of deep breaths, then said "let's do this," right before hitting start on his watch, and heading into the turn. Denny liked to float the turns so to speak, then power down the straightaways, but sometimes like now his adrenaline surged too much, and he had to dial the pace back a half a click in the last hundred meters. He finished the first rep in thirty-six seconds, a little too fast. The guy had left out, Denny noticed while slowly rounding the far turns, and the young girl was gone by now as well.

The second 200 meters went according to plan, in thirty-nine seconds. The third as well in thirty-nine, which was right about where he wanted to be, within a second of goal pace. Denny prided himself on being able to hit prescribed paces and felt like he was fairly adept at doing so, without having to check his watch much. The fifth 200 was nailed in thirty-eight seconds, and the sixth through ninth all within one second, plus or minus the target time. His companions for the evening, the two ladies, continued to chat and jog, seemingly unaware of or uninterested in what Denny was doing; he happened to start the ninth rep right as they were heading into the same turn. And perhaps as a means of unconsciously soliciting attention, he went through the line in thirty-six seconds, though such effort was met with a dry heave or two at its terminus.

By now the former small-town track star was thoroughly feeling the cumulative effects of the workout, as he wobbled a bit on weak kneed legs out of turn four, and secretly wished the pending stretch of orange synthetic rubber could stretch out a little further, before he got back to the white painted line, and the number one; at which point he would charge into the chasm yet again. By the time he would get on the back stretch his legs would feel like lead balloons, as he shot pleading glances ahead at the Mahoning Mountain, still visible through the shadow of the impending night. One more, God, one more he would beg, or pray. Denny waged war against his own body, and his own mind. On the last one he counted it down with almost each passing stride; fifty meters to go, forty, thirty, twenty-and then, it was blessedly over.

Denny very slowly jogged another lap, then came on around to his gear. He put back on his pants and heavier shirt, slung the backpack over a shoulder and exited the dark stadium. The ladies had left as well. Denny walked over to his car and chucked the backpack onto the passenger's seat, after taking a long drink of water and grabbing a Quest protein bar from the outer compartment. He decided to do his cool down run through town; Denny headed out through one of the school ground's entrance and exit ways, and on northward up Ninth Street. Denny took a few turns, and ran around the hospital complex, slowing down as he stared up at some of the lit windows of the seventh floor; he tried to pin point the exact window of Keith's room. Suzanne had told him yesterday that he would be there for another couple of weeks, in a long-term care program, but that he seemed to be doing better. He asked her then if she wanted to meet up and run soon, which she responded with a yes-Saturday morning at the D&L.

"Keep fighting Keith," Denny said quietly into the chilly night air, as he continued on up a steep hill that the cross-country team used to do repeats on, known simply as the hospital hill. He didn't blast up the hill tonight, nor was there an orange cone to circle around at the top.

He cruised the slight downhill on Coal Street all the way to Third Street, where he took a right at Saint Peter and Paul's Church, and on down another hill. The legs had loosened up, and the 200s had felt pretty good. Denny was about to cut down to South Second Street, when he remembered that his car was still parked out by the new high school. What's one more mile anyhow he thought; besides the moon and stars will keep good company on the dimly lit streets.

Denny loaded his duffel bag up with dirty clothes and drove over to the laundromat, located along route 443 next to two gas stations, and across the street from the Boulevard Restaurant, and Beacon Diner. Many times, Suzanne and Keith had practically insisted that he do his laundry at their house, Jennifer too. But Denny would always politely decline, instead opting to wash his clothes in the most curious of places, that he had become quite fond of. For over the course of the past few months he had learned to appreciate the gritty, lower class charm of the place, which served too as a reminder of some of the necessary trade-offs in his quixotic odyssey. The usual ensemble was present on any given day; the working poor, the young and drug addled, the outcast Hispanic minorities, or those on welfare and food stamps. And their omnipresent children, noisy and rambunctious, likely a result from an overabundance of sugar, and too much processed food in their diets. The itinerant runner blended right in.

After starting a load of laundry, Denny liked to belly up to the bar, in this case a long wooden counter in the front of the building, with wooden stools to sit on, and an unobstructed view of the street outside. 443 was one of the busier routes in town, and folks were always coming and going from the restaurants. Sometimes one of the local newspapers would serve as a chum, or the free monthly entertainment guide distributed in there on a rack against the one wall. Denny would stumble across names of people he used to know, from school, little league baseball, cub scouts, or from their old church. Occasionally it would surprise him that someone was still alive, like the old guy everyone called Bloomy, who hung around the baseball diamonds every spring and summer. They even had his picture in one of the papers a few weeks ago.

Or Denny would take out a notebook and attempt to do some sketching with a pencil, though he was quite bad at it, and did it more so to try and impress Jennifer with just how bad of an artist he really was. He perhaps exhibited a little more talent writing stream of conscience like poems, about the life he saw passing in and out of there. I should make it into one big piece he told Jennifer once, and the only place people could read it would be at the laundromat. Others could add to it, like collective free verse; he did add a most important stipulation, that in order to collaborate, one had to also do a load of laundry. "I could even come by and add pictures to it," Jennifer excitedly added.

"Yes!" said Denny, while adding that not before she also agreed to the terms of doing laundry there as well. Tonight, he sat there with a blank page in front of him, as the sound of spinning dryers droned on in the background.

Suzanne was already there and standing by her car when Denny pulled into the lot. She looked quite cold, so Denny tried to quickly get himself ready to run, which was not one of his strengths in the sport. "Morning," he called out as he got out of the car, while trying to get his Garmin watch strapped around two layers of long sleeves, then stashing his keys in the usual spot, inside the driver's side back tire.

"Hey Denny," she greeted him.

"I think I'm ready. Let’s do this."

"Dang it's cold." And it was cold, very cold beneath a thick bank of charcoal, grey clouds. There was a bit of a breeze too; coupled with the damp air it was downright raw outside. Several inches of snow were forecast, beginning late morning. Denny could almost taste it in the air, as the area's early springtime weather seemed to be but a far-off memory.

Even though he had gloves on Denny was shaking his hands to warm them, which Suzanne noticed. "Once again, I am reaping what I have sowed," he said.

"We got fooled into thinking spring was here to stay."

"Indeed. But I would like to see one last snowfall."

"I don't." The wind picked up just after Suzanne had made her position on the matter unmistakably clear. Coming off the waters of the Lehigh made it feel like an icy blast stinging their faces. The only recourse was to keep running; for dedicated runners like the two of them, there was no turning back once they had begun.

Though once the runners got past the water treatment plant and onto the gravel, conditions became a bit more tolerable;

the thicket of woods between them and the river helped break up the wind. Denny told Suzanne about his workout on the track, and how much he loved the new surface, and about all the miles and running in general he was getting in. And the core work, like the planks he would do while taking breaks from work, or on his lunch hour.

"I haven't done planks in a while. I need to start back."

"I got into them a few years ago. I used to do a lot of sit-ups but one of the coaches I'm friends with Andrea is a certified personal trainer and told me that they really don't do much for you. Sit-ups that is."

"Good to know."

"Yes. She makes us all pretty much want to weep sometimes in practices with all these sadistic core routines. Like writing out the alphabet with your legs extended and elevated off the ground while you lie on your back. Or these things called Russian twists while sort of sitting with your legs elevated out again. Then twisting back and forth while trying to stay stable. Or coming forward and throwing air punches as hard as you can." Denny was really caught up in it. "One night it reminded me of the movie 'Biloxi Blues.' When they were taking their time going to cross the river and Christopher Walken yelled out 'what would you do if the Japanese attacked?' And Matthew Broderick's character said 'surrender and get some sleep.'"

"That's the first time I have felt like laughing in weeks," Suzanne responded.

Yes, I can only imagine Denny thought. He asked, "so how is he now? How are you?"

"Keeps getting better. Slowly. He goes to therapy most of the day and has another counsellor as well. He said that seems to be helping him."

"That's good."

"Plus, one of the doctors there thinks that he may have PTSD. It was never diagnosed from back in the war when he got blown up in that tank."

"We can pin that on Saddam Hussein."

"Yes. We'll find out soon. He'll be there for a few more weeks I think. At least that's the plan for now," Suzanne said. The two of them ran for a while in silence. Denny started to look forward to seeing Jennifer later in the day; she got off of work at three, and her kids were at their father's house again until Monday.

"Let's turn around up here and do six miles."

"Okay," Denny agreed.

"I've run this every morning for the last thirteen days. I have a streak going."

"Wow that's awesome. Good for you."

Once they turned around and started to head back northward, Denny did a few elongated bounds; not only to help alleviate how cold he still felt, but to try and loosen up his hamstrings, which had been feeling a bit sore of late. "I swear the wind is in our face again. How can that possibly be?" Denny asked.

"I hate when that happens," Suzanne answered, though she seemed to take everything in stride, and battle through whatever conditions were thrown at her, in a silent, steeliness. She was tough as nails out here; that Denny already knew, but he had begun to see just how tough she must be the other twenty-three hours of the day too, as she explained how she was also managing full time employment and two kids, on top of all this other unfortunate stuff. He almost pleaded with her to let him help out in some way. She responded that he already was.

Denny sat on his lawn chair and watched the snow fall. He brewed up a cup of green tea and added honey and sat there with his legs propped on the window sill right next to the oil burning radiator, which was working much harder today. He sort-of slipped into a blissful trance while sipping the hot tea and watching all the puffy white flakes fall gently from the sky; Denny would follow individual flakes each taking their own unique path downward, until disappearing below him near the ground. The tea tasted a little sweet when it hit his lips and went into his mouth, before rolling smoothly down his throat and into his belly. All of his muscles were relaxed, like he had been tranquilized with an anesthetic. Denny could feel the tops of his eyelids almost infinitesimally begin to droop over his eye balls; his field of vision would decrease from the top.

He wasn't sure if he had dozed off a little, but the ring of his cell phone brought him back to full consciousness. It was Jennifer calling; she had just got back from stopping off at her mom's house and had the wonderful idea while driving home through the snow that they should go sledding over in the cemetery. She had two toboggans, and the backside of the cemetery had some good hills to slide down. "I'm in," Denny said into the phone.

It was the second time today that he had to get all bundled up. Denny headed out on foot; the snow was flying pretty steadily by now, he guessed two to three inches had already accumulated, and the forecast was now predicting six to eight inches in total. The wind was blowing menacingly strong from the north and east; the wind chill last read eight degrees on the WNEP weather app that Denny had downloaded on his phone. This is sort of nuts he thought. It would be April in less than a week. And this sledding business was sort of nuts as well. But so was Jennifer. Then again so am I, which is perhaps one of the big reasons they got along so well, Denny concluded. A snow plow coming up the street from the rear got Denny' attention; he hopped back over onto the sidewalks. Not many cars were out on the roads. Denny did love the snow, just not being real cold in it. He kept pulling the hood of his sweatshirt over top the beanie on his head, but the wind kept blowing it back off.

Denny caught sight of Jennifer coming down Fourth Street. She was bundled up as well, and had her head down looking at the ground as she briskly walked, while dragging two toboggans behind her. His spirits lifted when he saw her; he decided to cross over to the other side of the street down the road from her, and then took cover behind a parked car. Denny scooped up fresh snow from the ground and formed a snowball about the size of a softball, though he was careful not to pack it too tight. The snow was rather powdery and dry, which was unusual for a storm this late in the season. He peered out from behind the car and watched Jennifer as she labored along and waited until she was a little up ahead of him before firing the snowball at her. He missed, and apparently Jennifer was completely unaware she was being targeted, for she never broke stride, or took her eyes off the snowy pavement. So, Denny made another snowball and fired, this time hitting her on the side, making a dull thudding sound as snow splattered on her winter jacket.

"HEEYYYY"

But Denny was too quick for her as he ducked back down behind the car.

"Ok so this is how it’s going to be." Jennifer had stopped and was looking around for her assassin.

Denny surreptitiously made another snowball, waited a few seconds, then popped up and threw all in one motion. He missed, and in the process exposed his position.

"Ok Mister!" Jennifer bent over and began scooping up snow herself as Denny bounded across the street and stopped her before she had a chance to return fire.

"Too quick for ya," he said to her as he grabbed ahold of one of the toboggan's ropes.

"Too sneaky is more like it."

The two of them entered the cemetery through the main entrance gates and walked down one of the snow-covered macadam paths which led to the south end. The headstones were all covered in snow too. "This is so beautiful," Jennifer remarked. The Mahoning Mountain, which was less than a half mile in front of them, was almost entirely shrouded by the snowfall. The whole scene was like a winter wonderland; they stopped at the top of a steep hill which sloped away from the last row of tombstones. "All aboard," Jennifer announced, as she laid down head first into her toboggan.

"I haven't done this since I was a kid," Denny said as he boarded his own vessel.

And the sledding was crazy fun as they took their first run down the hill side by side. Good speed could be built on the upper half of the hill, and the snow pack wasn't too deep that the toboggans would sink in much and slow their momentum.

"That was righteous man," Jennifer exclaimed after they came to a stop at the bottom of the hill.

"Come here often?" Denny replied in a low, goofy voice as he pulled on her arm.

"Not in a while." She got out and started trudging back up. Denny followed, "We used to come here a lot, especially after the first year we moved by."

"Gotcha."

"Think the boys are getting too old for it. Well maybe not Toby. But he's getting to that age too where he's not into going to do things with his Mom." Jennifer was breathing a bit heavier as they neared their start line. Denny was a tad bit labored too.

"You need to have the borough put a lift in here."

"Yeah that would be nice."

They sledded down the hill a few more times. Back up again at the top Jennifer said, "ok. One more time. But this one is a race. Loser buys dinner."

"You're on."

Both of them this time took running starts and dropped the toboggans in front of themselves, then hopped on board in continuous motions, though Denny was worried for a split second that he had wrenched his left knee. When they got about half way down, and were moving at a healthy rate, he reached over and grabbed ahold of Jennifer's toboggan, which impeded her speed just enough for him to pull ahead by a couple lengths. "No!" she called out and added something further about him being a rotten cheater, while he slid his way to victory.

"No fair. You." Jennifer picked up snow with both hands and threw it at him.

"All's fair in love and competitive sledding."

"I don't know how you live with yourself there Defillipis."

"There's a certain nuance to it."

The snow continued to steadily fall and add to the white blanket covering the cemetery and the town, while the two of them walked on up to Jennifer's house. She made hot chocolate to warm their frigid bones. It was like being a kid again thought Denny, though his cocoa didn't have any tiny marshmallows floating on top. But it sure did hit the spot anyway.

Chapter 9

One-night Denny became involved in some kind of caper planned by Suzanne. All he knew going in was to show up at the hospital at seven o'clock sharp, but to wait outside, specifically behind the big sign and bushes which lined the far side of the main entrance way. And to also wear something he could run in, which wasn't too much of a wardrobe stretch. "I don't know what the hell they are up to," he told Jennifer. "I think they might be trying to break him out of the place!"

"I'm fairly certain he could just sign his own release. Unless it's an insurance thing," Jennifer pondered. "Do they need a getaway driver?"

"Maybe they expect me to haul him away on my back."

Denny did as he was instructed, and even got there a bit early to pook about in the parking lot, but nothing seemed out of the ordinary. Although what would, he had to ask himself? He said hi to two nurses who walked past him; one of them was friends with Jennifer. Denny jogged out to the road to get a better view of the top row of windows; almost all of them had lights on, including those that included where Keith's room had to be. A quick check of his watch revealed it was now 6:57. If I hear a fire alarm I know it's on Denny thought, as he scurried back over to his designated post, not before slyly casting numerous sideway glances.

The main entrance doors finally opened at almost precisely one minute past seven. Denny could hear the glass doors sliding horizontally, so he readied himself for action; an older lady with two young kids, a boy and girl walked by and into the parking lot. It was no-one from the Druckenmiller family. Denny kept checking his watch every fifteen, twenty seconds. There was another false alarm, then a third, as people continued to exit the main hospital building. It was now ten after seven; am I being punked Denny wondered? Someone must be filming all this, maybe Jennifer was even in on it? She's got a lot of connections here. And this could be payback for the treadmill incident. "What are these ruddy bastards up to?" Denny mused aloud into a sleeve of his sweatshirt.

Just then the door slid open again, and Denny heard a "hey," in the unmistakable voice of Keith. He was slowly running out into the parking lot. "Start moving," he instructed with a wave of his right arm to his somewhat bedeviled friend.

"Roger that," Denny replied. After all, he was always up for some good old-fashioned subterfuge, and a bit of risk. He broke into a light trot and followed Keith through the lot towards the road.

"Go right," he again instructed. "No talking yet," he added in an authoritative voice as they headed up the road, and then past another smaller building which housed doctors' offices but was closed for the night. Denny had no idea what was going on, though he did not want to break rank, so he remained silent and dutifully followed behind, half expecting a security guard or hospital administrator to leap out from the shadows at any moment to put an abrupt halt to whatever it was they were engaged in. Soon the two of them were on an adjacent road to the main hospital building, and out of visual sight from the entrance or parking lots. Keith slowed down; he was breathing pretty hard, though they had not been running that particularly fast. Hopefully, if any pursuit was engaged in a chase, they were not that fleet of foot either.

"How goes it?" Keith asked through exhaled breaths.

"Excellent. And you?"

"Good. Good. Thought maybe you could use some company. On an evening run. Around our fair little town tonight." Keith was smiling like a Cheshire cat.

I'll be damned thought Denny. The ruddy bastard snuck out of the place to go for a run. "For sure my friend," he replied. "For sure."

They slowly climbed the hospital hill up towards Coal Street, then took a right turn and proceeded into the heart of town, dimly lit by street lights, and fairly quiet save for some cars driving on the roads.

"So how did you pull this off?" Denny queried.

Keith started. "Well Sue brought up some running clothes thrown in a bag. If anyone asked, she was going to tell them it was books from home. She told the nurse on duty up there now, that I needed to talk to Ron and Nicole, in private. And didn't want to be disturbed. For about an hour." He took several shorter strides to regain his breathing better. "Then she left them sitting in there, on the side of the bed by the door. To sort of block any view from the door. While she waited down the hall, near the elevator. For the coast to be clear." The two of them got to Eighth Street and Keith once again motioned with his one arm, this time to indicate a right turn. "But some doctor was out there. So, we had to wait a bit. Sue texted Ron and then held the elevator. While I ran down the hall and jumped in."

"You guys should do prison breaks next."

"Let's hope it doesn't come to that." They ran down a big hill in silence for a short while; the only sounds in the dark were that of their shoes hitting the macadam of the road. It was a clear, beautiful night, and temperatures had warmed up nicely again after the snowfall the previous weekend. Spring seemed again to be just around the corner; that perpetual time of rebirth, rejuvenation. Interposed with resplendent colors, and sweet fragrances.

Keith started the conversation back up. "I laid there one night after you came to visit. And thought about what you said. Well not right away, it was many nights later. Anyhow, about the running and all that. I mean why not? I remembered back to when I used to do it a lot more regularly. Like when you were living back here after college. Things did seem better then. Granted circumstances were much different. But things will always be changing right? That's something for sure. But I guess I never made the connection between how I felt inside, with what I was doing out here. And I guess I have nothing to lose at this point, either right?"

"And much to gain," Denny added.

"For sure. So, I needed to get out here and feel this again. Recall what it's like. Even if I'm dying anytime I go up a hill." Keith laughed a bit, and they ran on, crossing Mahoning Street. "You know I listen to what you say. Most of the time at least. Some of it to me is a bit mumbo jumbo. Like the god stuff. Not that I discount it. But I'm not sure there. Though I can see how it works for you. Sometimes the perspectives are just so different."

"True."

"But I need something to ground me. Some kind of stability. A connection too. To something bigger than the dumb everyday stuff. And I don't want to just be fed medication all day. Though some of it has really helped. Not sure where I am headed here."

"Down South Eight Street."

“No, what I'm trying to say. You get it right?"

"I do. I hear they got you going to a lot of therapy and counseling in there."

"Yes. Several hours a day. Writing in journals too. All fairly labor intensive this long-term recovery program I'm enrolled in."

"Sounds like it."

"I need it. But also need something that I can get out here for myself. This sort of reprieve where I know I'm doing something positive. I can't stay locked up forever. Nor would I want to. I need to be challenging myself again like I used to. Especially if I feel like I'm going to slip into a darker place. I'd love to even get back to doing some races again. Been years. All about finding a healthy balance, and alternatives to self-destructive, darker tendencies. That's something we talk about in group all the time."

"Makes sense."

"Let's cut over to Ninth Street and loop back up. I can't stay out here all night." The streets were almost pitch black where they were in a more remote enclave of town. Denny guessed they had been running for about twenty minutes, maybe twenty-five. He never had started his watch. "Wow I'm out of shape," Keith said as they started up another hill.

A few moments later Denny spoke up, he was hesitant to say too much tonight. "Remember what I said that first run we did together? When I first came back? That if it weren't for running I would have put a bullet in my head?"

"Sounds like something you'd say."

"I once heard a guy I knew at the time who skated say basically the same thing. That he would have shot himself if it weren't for his skateboard. Surfers too, though that one example was a first-person account. And I'm sure this could be applied to numerous activities."

"Yes."

"It helps me to keep the darker tendencies at bay too, as you so eloquently put it. There's still a part of me deep inside that wants to self-destruct. Blow it all to hell and gone. If I may paraphrase Soundgarden."

"This hill is bringing out. Some dark tendencies. In me."

"It's freaking great isn't it?" Denny almost yelled. The faint smile that spread across Keith's face acknowledged his agreement, as he plodded up the remaining stretch of the hill. It was great. It was better than great if that was possible. On nights such as this, anything did seem possible. The two runners both knew it to be true, without any need for verbal affirmation. Denny prayed as they ran that the running Gods would take care of Keith, and continue to shepherd him into the light, as they had, and continued to do so for himself. Later as he watched his friend re-enter the hospital, he knew they both had many more miles to run before either of them slept.

The days seamlessly moved on into the middle of spring. The temperatures continued to warm, and the landscape continued to transform itself from the dull, drab browns and greys of winter, to the greens, whites, and yellows indigenous to April and May. The rains that came only seemed to accentuate nature's annual spring colors. Denny continued to pile up the mileage, knocking out runs six, seven days a week, and completing the hard workouts with the seriousness of a child at play, even embracing the occasional setbacks as opportunities for growth; seeing them as gentle reminders to continue to develop patience and humility, and to allow God's will to unfold on a daily basis.

He was feeling a little more devout, reading whatever he could get his hands on about faith and spirituality, or conversing more with people like Suzanne who was a practicing Catholic. All three of them even ran one Saturday morning, that is Denny, Suzanne, and Keith, who had been released from the long-term care facility at the hospital and was living back in his home again.

Trent would meet up with Denny at times as well, usually on the D&L. On a particular evening the two of them met up with Carla by chance and ended up running a good bit of her ten-miler with her, while swapping some stories and reminisces about days long since passed, but definitely not forgotten. Denny and Trent wished her good luck in her marathon, where she was hoping to break four hours again. And which she eventually did, clocking in at a hair over three hours and fifty minutes; also, a new PR.

Denny even convinced Jennifer to run outside with him one evening on the towpath, and he was pleasantly surprised that they were able to get almost three miles in; longer than she had ever run before, or so she thought. "Man. I can see how you totally get high off this," Jennifer exclaimed, as they sat down under the shelter by the parking lot. "Though I think I'll stick to my spinning in the gym."

"I think someone has just earned themselves an ice cream cone."

"Or a couple of pints."

And so it went with Jennifer. Ecstatically in love again, almost twenty years later. However, truth be told, below the smooth surface of it all lurked some major decisions, that by necessity would have to be made, but for now the subject was never directly broached, though casual hints dropped at times by both parties did foreshadow the eventual inevitability of it all. But as Denny took Jennifer's hand and led her across the gravel lot to the car, all of that seemed like something from a far-off galaxy.

A few nights later Trent and Denny stopped off outside the high school track and field complex. They had just completed a hilly seven-mile run out into Mahoning Township and back. The old teammates stood behind the fence off turns three and four and watched as what had to be more than a hundred and fifty elementary and middle school kids in every measure of size and ability ran, jumped, and threw implements. Both of them would scan around and search out kids whom they felt had some sort of resemblance to the kids that they had competed with and against, back when they were practicing on the very same teams, all those years before. It was a comical little exercise to undertake, and Denny even found a few kids that could quite possibly be a younger version of himself, or Trent out there. Running lap after lap, wanting to get just one more in to impress the coach before the end of practice. Jennifer's two sons were in the mix somewhere, as were Keith and Suzanne's kids. After a few minutes the two of them headed on out, unnoticed by any of the youthful stars of the current day, which as Trent said to Denny, was exactly the way it should be.

Friday evening arrived, and Denny was ready to bust out the door after the completion of another work week; plus, the weather had been tantalizing him all day, as temperatures had soared into the seventies, coupled with warm breezes that carried the smells of spring on through open windows, and into his domicile. He took off up South Second Street, then down towards the Weissport Bridge.

As Denny crossed over he looked down at the Lehigh River, which looked healthy and robust from all the heavier rains that had fallen of late. The trees lining her banks were starting to show ample proof that they would be in full bloom very soon; hundreds and thousands of greenish yellow buds covered all the branches. Shorts and a tank top was the chosen attire, along with a backwards baseball cap that covered some of his now long, wavy blond hair. Sunglasses shielded his eyes from the still bright sun. Denny crossed the rail road tracks and headed up Main Road and out into Franklin Township.

He followed Main Road as it wound its way eastward, gradually away from the more populated areas near town, into the verdant, rolling farmlands, replete with the strong odor of manure in the air, as the planting season was occurring in earnest. Denny ran steady, but not too hard. He always loved the Friday evening runs when he was on a standard Monday through Friday work schedule; he was free, so to speak, for about the next two and a half days.

Denny crossed Harrity Road and passed Platz's restaurant and got onto Beltzville Road, then passed the large marina and bait shop, and eventually on by these wooden horse stables where his old friend Avery from track and cross country, used to keep her horses. She lived on a ranch in Oklahoma now, and raised all kinds of livestock. Denny smiled at the memory of her; she was a real tenacious runner back in school, and a real free spirit too.

The road narrowed before ending at the breast of the dam. It was a massive, steeply sloped pile of orange and brown colored tightly packed rock and dirt, that covered the interior concrete structure of the dam itself. When he was younger, Denny often thought about what an incredibly difficult workout it would be to do hill repeats on the thing. Though it was fenced off and marked against trespassers, regardless of their intentions. Instead Denny found the trailhead to a seldom used, somewhat secret trail that cut into the thick woods, and through a ravine, at the bottom of which was a rapidly flowing, wide stream that emptied into the Pohopoco Creek.

The forest was predominately pine trees, which kept the environment much cooler and damp, and not well lit. The single-track trail's surface was mostly grass and dirt, or pine straw in some sections. The sweet smell of pine sap was quite pungent as well in certain areas. He could hear the gurgling rush of water and catch glimpses of the stream through the overgrown vegetation, though in spots the stream formed larger pools of water, before cascading through openings that created miniature rapids around larger, mossy rocks that protruded out of the surface.

About a mile in, Denny crossed to the other side by getting onto another trail that was no wider than a deer trace, and angled beneath an almost hidden bridge, on a road that headed to the main entrance of the state park, a few more miles to the east. The trail then snaked sharply up the side of the ravine, until it was a good thirty or forty meters above the stream. For some reason he thought of the movie "Field of Dreams," and the scene where one of the baseball players, being mesmerized by the natural beauty of his surroundings, asks Kevin Costner if this is heaven? "No. It's Iowa," was the response. As Denny picked his way gingerly along the faint trail, carefully stepping on top of, or over exposed tree roots, with the melodic songs of birds emanating from the woods, he felt a bond with that old ball player, for each step was like being in some kind of ethereal paradise of his own. As the breezes occasionally danced around the trees and playfully tingled his skin, he could almost swear he heard that same mysterious voice as well, saying, "go the distance."

Chapter 10

Back home, and back over in town, some changes appeared on the horizon. Keith had finally found tenants for the apartment Denny was living in, and they would be moving in shortly. This was of course expected at some point in time, and Denny was grateful that he had been granted the sanctuary for as long as he was and told Keith he would help him clean the place up and assist in the addition of a new layer of a paint in the kitchen and bathroom before moving out the following week. Keith told Denny that he could also show his gratitude by continuing to hold him accountable to his running, which of course he said he would be more than happy to do. Good fortune did not immediately desert Denny though, as his old friend Jerry, through another mutual friend, was able to get him a very sweet deal on an extended month's stay in a room at the Hampton Inn hotel, off of route 209 in Franklin Township.

That next Saturday Denny moved into his new temporary home on the first floor of the Hampton Inn. Fortunately, the move itself was not that difficult nor physically taxing; one benefit of not having a whole heck of a lot of things in tow. "Nice," he exclaimed after he had signed some paperwork in the hotel's office and had been given two swipe card keys and entered the room. The room was rather large for a hotel room and consisted of a living room nook in one corner, and a separate sort of office like area with a desk which he could work at, and plenty of open space to do all his ancillary strength and core work.

A king-sized bed was in the back of the room, next to the bathroom which was down a short hallway. And of course, there was a television; a thirty-four-inch flat screen setting on top of an entertainment stand. Though mostly out of circumstance, he had learned to do without a television set the past several months. Change is good he pondered, while he began to unpack his clothes and separate them into the various drawers of the large dresser. Then Denny changed into some running clothes and headed out one of the doors on the backside of the hotel; he wasn't going to go too far today, so as to not miss out on the complimentary breakfast, served daily in the dining room next to to the lobby.

He knocked out a hilly six-mile run, which began with climbing the long winding hill behind the hotel on Rock Street, which at its crest went thru a densely wooded area well above where the Pohopoco Creek widened out, before eventually flowing into the Lehigh River about two miles downstream. Some scattered houses were back in there as well; one of them belonged to this kid he had known in elementary school named Robbie Steigerwalt, who got hit in the head by a lawn dart in second or third grade, which required half of his hair to be shaved off and left a several inches long gash of a scar where emergency surgery had to be done. Denny had vague memories of going up here to his house, probably to birthday parties or something.

He took on a few more quad busting hills after Rock Street, before returning back to the hotel in under fifty minutes. Denny snagged a copy of the weekend edition *USA Today* newspaper from a table in the lobby and poured himself a cup of coffee from one of the large, heated thermoses, before heading back to his room. Out the windows of his room were a view of the now lush, dark green, rolling hills and small mountains stretching northward to Jim Thorpe and beyond. He did his post run Myrtl routine, took a quick shower, and briefly checked out the rest of the hotel amenities before going to breakfast. There was a nice sized indoor pool, in a room that sort of resembled a greenhouse, next to a gym that had a couple of treadmills, spin bikes, an elliptical machine, and a universal weights machine. A man was running on one of the treadmills and watching CNN on a television set, which hung down from near the top of the back wall.

One of the women working in the kitchen said hello to Denny while maneuvering her way through the dining hall's back room, where all the food and beverages were located. He eagerly filled a plate up with scrambled eggs, bacon, sausage links, and French Toast slices. There was also a large bowl of fruit situated on one of the counter tops, another bowl with various flavors of yogurt resting in ice, and a big cereal contraption with four separate plastic containers filled with different brands. There was also a waffle maker. And a juice machine. This place has it all he said to himself, before finding a secluded table up against the wall. Denny slowly ate and read the newspaper, while periodically watching people come and go. A big flat screen television tuned to ESPN was mounted on the opposite wall above a fireplace. Denny texted the particulars to Jennifer who was at work. A bit later she replied, "Jealous!!!"

A week or two later Denny did hit a bit of a rough patch with his running. Nothing major, but he felt himself becoming lethargic, less enthused about the daily runs, and he started to feel a tad overwhelmed trying to continually hit certain weekly mileage totals. It had been building for a short time, but Denny had tried to somewhat ignore the doubts creeping in, for he had staked so much to this quest, that he feared what would become of him without it all. And the actual workouts themselves, when looked at by Denny in the Jack Daniel's book, would give him almost a nauseating feeling of impending doom, knowing what lie in store for him that coming evening on the roads, or the towpath, or the D&L Trail.

One solution was to knock the harder runs out in the morning, but then he would become disconsolate the previous evening about how early he was going to have to set his alarm. A particular workout Denny cut short; 1200-meter VO2max intervals, that he was attempting to run on the towpath. On this specific run, he just did not feel like he had the mental strength needed to endure the physical pain being produced by running well under a six minute per mile pace. "The hell with it," he angrily muttered as he eased off the pace, while gasping for air and feeling like he was about to dry heave. Intuitively Denny also knew it shouldn't have felt quite that hard, for it was something he had successfully completed before.

Back in the hotel room he had scrawled in his notebook, "I'm cracking up, becoming weak, unable to push through the pain. My true self is being revealed, yet again." Ever the burgeoning perfectionist when it came to his chosen sport, Denny went through a mental checklist to try and pin point the roots of his distress. Changes in diet, sleep, temperament? Or training volume, intensity, density? Maybe it was just the warmer temperatures having such an effect on his performance.

Later he texted Charlie back in North Carolina about his quandary. A reply came back to essentially chill, relax, and take a few days off; you won't lose any fitness either he stated. Of course, Denny knew all of that, but like just about every other runner he knew, he was stubborn to a fault. It was always much easier to give sensible advice to others, than to practice it oneself. Another text popped up a minute or two later, "and when the hell are you coming back?"

"Good question," was the reply sent back. It was a question weighing much more heavily on Denny's mind each and every passing day, or so it seemed. The deal he received at the hotel would only last for a thirty-one-day period, and after that it would not be financially rational for him to stay in the place any longer, especially when he considered the fact that he was also still paying rent on his condo down at the beach. Which he realized after such a prolonged absence from, that he missed; not the residence per se, but living on an island, less than a quarter of a mile from the ocean itself. Denny looked at the calendar; by the end of next week he would have been gone from North Carolina, and up here in Pennsylvania for five months. Wow he thought, time can have a subtle way of playing tricks on us, can't it? Maybe he had just become a little too high on the hog with all of this as well? And then there was Jennifer-

A few days later it occurred to Denny that perhaps this running funk was a sign that his work up north was coming to an end. He deliberated that and a few other things while sitting on top of a cement wall behind the back-parking lot of the hotel. It was a picturesque, soothing late spring twilight-almost perfect, he thought, as he gazed out at the hills and mountains to the north, part of the terrain which formed the outdoor environment he had spent twenty plus years of his life in. The moon was almost full as it rose into the sky, which was mostly dark, except for some purple and pink hues in the west. A gentle breeze delicately swirled the leaves on all the trees nearby, as Denny dangled his legs off the wall, and sipped on a cup of hot chamomile tea he had made in the hotel lobby. He felt at peace with his surroundings, at peace with the road he had taken, and the roads yet to be travelled. "You have welcomed me back into your bosom, fed and nourished me, brought joy to tearful eyes, let me hear the sweet airs of laughter, allowed me to love and be loved, when you laid a gentle hand on my shoulder, and bathed me in the holy waters of life." Denny was feeling poetic, as he looked up at the twinkling stars above.

That Saturday, after Denny had killed an eleven-mile run which validated the benefits of taking some much-needed rest, he and Jennifer drove out to the Christman Trails to go hiking. They parked in a small parking lot by the trailheads, located about five miles east of the dam, and plunged into the deep, damp old growth forest that surrounded Beltzville Lake. "Into the heart of darkness," Denny proclaimed as they began walking down a steep incline on the trail that led over to the waterfalls, one his favorite places to explore growing up.

"I should come out here to paint. This is so beautiful."

"I'm still in a state of disbelief that you have never once been out here in these environs."

"I've lead a sheltered life." Jennifer squeezed his hand when she said that, as the trail fell off sharply, and was just about wide enough for the two of them to walk side by a side through the woods, a mix of deciduous and coniferous trees. They crossed a small wooden foot bridge which spanned a stream, then climbed back up the other side of the narrow gorge.

"It's just up ahead," Denny said quietly, as the sound of rushing water became audible.

"Ohh."

For years Denny's family, and the Hackenberg family, who were longtime friends, would come out here a couple of times a year to hike all over the network of trails along the north side of the lake. In total four adults and six kids made for quite the hiking party;

they would go for miles at a time wandering all throughout the woods, chomping occasionally on nuts and raisins, or granola bars, and drinking water out of canteens. John Muir perhaps smiled down upon them; to this day Denny still loved being out of doors, where he felt more comfortable and connected to the world around him, perhaps a little more in tune with the person he sought to be. Some of his favorite authors like Emerson, Thoreau, and Gary Snyder all worshipped at the altar of mother nature.

The trail dropped down again through some larger boulders, perhaps left there from the end of the ice age. Denny led Jennifer out onto a rocky outcropping about half way down the cascading falls, and off to the one side where they could sit and enjoy the view, created by a wide stream that fell several times from one shelf of rocks to the next; about a thirty or forty-foot drop in total. A deep pool of water formed right near where they were, and another one by the base of the falls. "Careful, this moss is slippery as heck," he cautioned Jennifer, as he took both of her hands and guided her out close to the water's edge.

"This is so beautiful."

"Just like you."

"Oh Denny." She kissed him on the cheek as they sat huddled together on the top of a gigantic rock. For a while the two of them just sat there not saying anything, each submerged in their own thoughts, or lack of thoughts, as the water rushed rapidly on downward, drowning out much of anything else except the louder calls of some birds high up in the trees that drooped overhead. It was a roaring silence which could cut like a diamond; an almost mystical power, which Denny liked to imagine himself being able to harness and store, and let lie latent in his own psyche, until it was time to unleash all of it when running, or writing. Perhaps Jennifer was absorbed in her own process of creativity, as her eyes watched the water continue to flow in a never ending, enchanted dance.

"What's going to happen to us?" she asked.

"We'll be ok. Just don't lean too far out over the rocks." Denny wasn't mute to the tone in her voice, it had struck him like a thunderbolt. But old habits die hard, and confronting emotional dilemmas remained a weakness of his.

"Maybe I already have." Jennifer paused briefly, then added, "two can play at this game."

She could disarm him as quickly as that and render him speechless. He, who seemed never to be at a loss for a witty comeback, an ironic rejoinder, was left somewhat hapless when it came to matters of the heart, especially with someone like Jennifer, who held such sway over his entire wellbeing. Had he only known all those years ago when out at these falls that a scene like this was going to take place, he could have sought some wisdom from those who had lived through half a lifetime or more of a whole range of experiences. When he was with Jennifer though he felt like that young kid again; sheltered perhaps, from some of the messiness of the big old ugly world. But he would have to go straight through this; he knew it was coming. They both knew it was coming. Perhaps it’s why he had brought her out there today.

"Come on Denny," she asked with more emotion than he had maybe ever heard in her voice. Denny took his hand and lovingly moved some of her golden, brown hair behind her ear; at that moment in time she had never looked so radiantly alluring, so alive and real, that it almost overwhelmed his senses. Scattered beams of sunlight poked through the canopy of trees, one of which seemed to illuminate Jennifer's face. Perhaps he was just imagining it.

"I wish we could sit here like this forever and ever, and everything would just take care of itself. Like it does in a fairy tale. You are my enchanting princess."

"And you my handsome prince."

"But I suspect as lovely as that concept is, that it's somehow not quite feasible. Though I've always been somewhat of a foolish dreamer." They both looked upwards at the spray being created from the water falling off the upper shelf of rocks. The breeze picked up and moved the tree branches a little, allowing for shafts of light to penetrate down into the mist, which created a speckled splatter of rainbow like colors.

"Me too," Jennifer whispered into Denny's ear, as she clasped his hand and leaned her head onto his shoulder. "I love you. Always."

"I love you. No matter what," he replied while turning to look into her eyes, those very eyes that took his breath away back on that cold winter night, which seemed like forever ago. Those same eyes that he would gaze into all those years before and lose himself inside her soul. Denny could feel his heart beating inside of his chest, as they continued to sit so close together beside the falls. He knew without knowing what was next, and he knew that Jennifer knew too. After a while he suggested a hike on the upper trail that led to the lake, about a mile and half away. It would give them ample time to talk. Jennifer agreed. And perhaps like Emerson had once written, Denny too never trusted a sedentary thought.

The trail wound deeper into the forest, well away from any semblance of civilization, which made the ecosystem feel almost primitive and virgin, similar to where Denny ran occasionally along the Switchback Trail near Mauch Chunk Lake, as he had done last weekend with Trent. Jennifer remarked how she could get lost in here for days, maybe weeks? She also vowed to bring her boys out soon.

"I can still recall certain landmarks out here, or very specific views of the lake. Some of the inlets that cut back away from the main body of water," Denny said. He had one particular image in mind of a small grassy meadow on the side of short, but steep hill near the end of one of the other trails they all used to hike on. Why this image remained burned into his brain he did not know.

"That's amazing after all this time. You have a really good memory."

"I never realized the impact this place had on me until years later I would think about it. I came out here after my Mom had died. The other family's mom had passed away years before. This place just seemed like as good as any to honor their memories or something. I guess sometimes we have to return all the way back to the roots of things to be able to see that."

"Well I never went anywhere so I wouldn't know." In Jennifer's voice there was a touch of sadness, perhaps a little regret, all coupled with a trace of terse acknowledgement of the differences between the two of them, which was a big factor as to why they stood at the crossroads they found themselves at. Both of them continued to evade talking more directly about the subject at hand. Personally, Denny would rather run quarters around a track until he vomited, then to attempt to articulate in person what he was feeling, especially when he was conflicted and flummoxed by the reality of a particular situation. He could be real selfish at times, and being in relationships, even those not of the romantic type, always brought forth such negative characteristics. But this couldn't be postponed, not a second longer.

Denny stopped on the trail and once again took both of Jennifer's hands in his. A little gust of wind swept down again from atop the trees, which blew some of her hair in front of her face. He leaned in and tried to blow all the strands away from her eyes. "Hey there," he stammered a little.

"Hey yourself."

"I pray all the time. For guidance, for things in life mostly. Asking for help. And giving thanks." The woods seemed to hush as the breeze subsided; the trees appeared to lean inward a slight bit as if to listen more intently, and bear witness to the testimony. Two squirrels skittered after each other up a tree behind Jennifer. Denny was keenly aware of their presence.

"Truth is I don't know what to do. About us. I wish maybe that I did but I don't. I feel like I'm in some kind of fantasy, though it's one that I can kind of pull back from and also look at from a certain distance and objective perspective. It's so wonderful now, but where does it go?" He swayed her arms in a swinging motion back and forth. She looked so vulnerable, so human standing before him. As he imagined he did as well, for it all tugged on Denny's heart. In his self-proclaimed vision quest, he never expected something like this to happen, not here, not now. But it had and was happening. Another person's heart was on the line too.

"I know. I think you put some words on it that I couldn't seem to find," Jennifer said, her voice quivering with raw emotion, and her eyes moist with tears. "Oh Denny," she said as she pulled him close and hugged him. Again, Denny flashbacked to that cold winter night.

Jennifer pulled back and quickly wiped her eyes. "You have a life elsewhere. I know that. My truth is that I am kind of jealous of that. You got away from here a long time ago and I'm happy for you."

"It doesn't mean all that much."

"Yes, it does," she replied a little more emphatically. "We all used to talk about going places and living, starting new lives in different spots and you actually did it. Not many do. Be proud of that."

"I feel like I have two homes. One here and one in North Carolina. Either I am real lucky, or it means I don't have a true home. Maybe that doesn't make sense. I'm sorry."

"Don't be sorry with me. Ever." A smile returned to her face. "My world is my boys here. They are the most important thing ever to me. I kind of lost sight of that the past few months. So, we both have our things you see."

"I do. They are so lucky to have you." Denny asked if she wanted to walk a little further; there was a real cool overlook of the lake up ahead.

As they walked onward Jennifer talked about all the times she used to dream about moving somewhere far off, like out west in the desert to Arizona or New Mexico. In fact, she had started looking for nursing jobs in Tucson and Santa Fe, but around the same time she got involved with her ex-husband, and before she knew it they were married and had a first child on the way. And slowly but surely that part of her died off inside as the years went by, although she did like raising her kids here, and looking back it was the best thing that ever happened to her, in spite of all the hardships and suffering. Maybe one day when they are grown and out on their own I'll head off somewhere she speculated, as the two of them crested a small hill, and the deep bluish, green colored lake became partially visible through the pine trees up ahead.

Denny understood. He admired her determination to provide her children the best possible life that she could, especially in light of how the family had tragically fallen apart. Once he had asked her why she didn't have her husband arrested after all he had done to her? Jennifer had explained that for the sake of the boys she had decided not to, as she did not want them growing up having a father who was in prison. She could not handle the thought of how that would affect them; not only not having his presence in their life, but also the stigmatism they'd have to endure once such facts became known in the community. As a condition of being granted partial custody, he had to continue to attend anger management therapy.

Jennifer had shown him the small cross attached to a thin necklace that she always wore but kept tucked inside her clothes. And explained how she would repeat the Lord's Prayer over and over again, until the concept of, "as we forgive those who trespass against us," was seared into her spirit and became a means for her own salvation. The notion that Jennifer would not put her children's needs in front of hers in anything that might ever transpire between the two of them, was something that Denny did not doubt for a second, even if it wasn't something being consciously processed all the time by him. And he knew she was real tough, a lot tougher than perhaps he had ever been.

The two of them sat down on top of the soft bed of pine needles carpeting the ground and looked down at the lake below. A boat drifted ever so slowly along. "Bet those people would never even guess that we are up here watching them," Jennifer said.

"We are like spies," Denny replied in the dry, rather matter of fact voice he liked to use. Jennifer burst out laughing.

"Great! You just blew our cover," he chided her.

"Get down behind the tree," she said, and then yanked him over on his side.

"Uh yeah." They both laid there on the ground, peeking around the pine tree right in front of them at the boat in the middle of the tranquil lake, which was much narrower across this far away from the breast of the dam. Eventually the boat drifted out of their sight.

"Coast is clear," Jennifer stated.

Denny pulled two Clif Bars out from a short's pocket and held them out in front of Jennifer. "Do you prefer blueberry crisp, or white chocolate macadamia nut?"

"That's a tough decision man."

"Okay. I'll make it for you," he said as he handed her the white chocolate bar.

"Good call."

"I thought so too."

Later at the hotel Denny sprawled out on the couch, and lazily flipped through the channels on the television. He found a Phillies game on and decided to watch some baseball. During the next inning he got up and went to the vending machines located half way down another hallway; he purchased a sixteen-ounce bottle of Dr. Pepper, a bag of bacon flavored hot fries, and a bag of red licorice. It's been quite a day, I deserve it, he rationalized after making his choices, and carrying the drink and snacks back to his room.

Jennifer and he agreed to avoid any big tearful goodbye scenes when he left to go back down South in less than two weeks. No, it wasn't their style; there was no sense staining something which had been so wonderfully intoxicating for the both of them, for after all they had captured lightning in a bottle this second go around, and this time could part ways amicably, with a deep love and respect for each other. And they both agreed that when it came to matters of the heart between them, that it would be a folly to permanently close any doors. It was likely the best possible hand that could have been collectively played, from the deck of cards they had been drawing from.

A couple of days later after the hike and talk, Denny received an email in his inbox from his sister Lilly in Virginia. He hadn't spoken to or heard from her since around Easter, but that wasn't necessarily out of the norm. But he was intrigued by the contents, and also a bit worried as to any bad news it could contain therein. He opened it up on his laptop and started to read about how the company she was working for was going to be one of the primary sponsors at the Richmond Marathon that fall, and as such she had been given two free entries to the race and wanted to know if Denny was interested in them and wanted to come there and do it. Plus, her and her husband had moved into a new house, and he and whomever he brought with, were more than welcome to stay there for the weekend. And that either of them would likely die if they attempted to run more than three miles. The email concluded with the question, "are you up for the challenge?"

Denny grinned as he reread the message. Gosh even my own sister knows how to motivate me he thought. "Yes. Challenge accepted," he wrote back. "And thanks!" And that was that, as apparently Denny had just agreed to run a marathon in a few months, something he had not done in several years. I'll figure it all out later he told himself, as he sat back down and logged into work for the day. Though the morning seemed to drag, as Denny's mind kept wandering back to the email, and the marathon.

On his lunch break he went onto the marathon's website, which had the banner, ‘America's friendliest marathon,’ emblazoned across the top; this amused Denny, as he glanced at pictures of smiling runners running down a tree lined boulevard, while enthusiastic looking bystanders cheered them on. But when scrolling through the website, something else caught Denny's eye; 18% of the finishers on average qualified for the Boston Marathon.

He leaned back in his chair and clasped his hands behind his head; the wheels had definitely begun to grind into motion. Plus, he knew just the person he would ask to go run the race with him.

That evening Denny headed out of the hotel, crossed over the hi-way, then ran down Main Road to the entrance of the towpath. The parking lot was nearly filled with vehicles; now that it was almost summer, more and more people were taking advantage of the towpath, and the D&L Trail for that matter. Good for all of them, Denny thought, but he preferred both when they were much less populated.

So instead of running on the towpath, he decided to cross the bridge into town, and get himself a good hill workout in. But to do something different, he formulated a plan on the fly to stay only in the alleys and avoid any of the regular streets if possible. Which is what he did, blasting fairly hard up each encountered hill, and recovering on the subsequent down hills, while passing all kinds of garages and garbage cans, as he zigzagged through several parts of the town, even running up the alley behind the house he had stayed at for all those prior months. A line from Lionel Ritchie kept playing in his head, "we were running in the shadows...," but he couldn't recall anything else from the song, though he knew it had nothing to do with the sport. The miles seemed to fly by; he even blessed a few stray cats. "Even unto the least," he said aloud to a mangy looking, orange cat.

In his hotel room that night Denny picked up the phone and called his old pal Bert down in North Carolina. He had run many marathons, including Boston two or three times. One year they had both run the Wrightsville Beach Marathon and had gone on some training runs together with a group of people. Denny finished in 3:16, the fastest of the two he had run, though he had sort of patched some training information together from online sources, and through conversations with people like Bert. He knew he could do better and wanted to be as prepared as he could be; after looking up the Boston Marathon qualifying times, Denny saw that he had to be under 3:15 to get into the prestigious event. Though he knew from listening to those in running circles, that in order to be actually accepted into the race one had to achieve a time a couple of minutes under their standard.

He got Bert on the line and explained all that to him and told him in brief about all the running he been doing up in Pennsylvania as well, and that he was looking for any advice he could offer, or what good training plans out there that he recommended following. Bert told him to order a book called *Advanced Marathoning* by Pete Pfzinger, and to follow one of the eighteen-week plans contained within. That's what he had used for his past two marathons, and it seemed to have worked out quite well, evidenced by a PR he had run in Myrtle Beach this past March, even breaking the coveted three-hour barrier.

"Look me up when you get back to the beach. We'll get some training runs in. I need some motivation myself right now."

"Sure thing Bert. Thanks amigo." Denny hung up the phone and went online to Amazon's website and ordered the book. He pulled out a calendar from the desk and counted off the weeks backwards from the race date in early November; about twenty-two and a half weeks stood between now, and then. He sat down on the reclining chair by the windows and gazed outside; it was dark out, as some cars drove up and down the hi-way out front. He recalled something long since forgotten, a little nugget of information that had been buried in some dusty, far corner of his mind. His Dad had once run a marathon in three hours and ten minutes, which periodically he would refer to as the DeFillipis' family record, of which he was quite proud to be in possession of; albeit at the time he was the only one in the family who had ever actually run a marathon. Nonetheless it was a pretty good running achievement, and respectable record, that had stood now for about thirty years. Denny chewed on this as he made out the silhouettes of the hills to the north. "You son of a bitch," he said, while continuing to stare out the window, "I'm coming after you."

Denny walked down to the side hallway and swiped his key to enter the indoor pool area. He jumped in and went for a swim. The water was warm and felt nice and soothing on his tired and achy muscles, especially when he stopped moving and just sort of floated in the water. The moon and stars were visible through the glass roof overhead, it was an aquatic paradise only a hundred feet or so from Denny's front door. For some reason he had not used the pool at all until tonight and thought that he must tell Jerry to bring Kayla over one night before he left out, since she loves to swim. After soaking in the water, and swimming a little more, he climbed up the steps at the shallow end and toweled himself off, then stopped off in the lobby to make himself a cup of tea, choosing a raspberry hibiscus flavor from the decorative wooden box. All of this he knew, was about to come to an end.

Denny ran into town and over to the Druckenmiller's house to go for a run with Keith. Ron was in the front yard with one of the dogs, trying to get the old Lab named Zia to jump up and down with him on the trampoline. While Nicole stood outside the netting of the contraption with a look of skepticism on her face.

"Jump higher," Denny offered. "And smile. Show her it's fun."

"She won't do it," said Nicole.

"Maybe you are crowding her. Or making her nervous. Step out for a minute," Denny said to Ron.

"Come on Zia jump," Ron tried again, to no avail.

"Hey Ronnie I have some good news for your Dad," Denny said, but Ron either didn't hear him, or didn't feel like responding, as he climbed out of the trampoline. Zia quickly followed him out.

Keith walked out the side door carrying his running shoes in his hands and asked his kids if they had finished washing out the floor of the garage. To which they both sort of mumbled and slouched off to the back yard; Zia followed behind.

"She's fifteen now. Really slowed down. Pretty much deaf too."

"That explains it. Wanna do the Uke's run? Or convalescent home?"

"Ukes sounds good." Keith ducked back inside the house and returned a few seconds later. Then they were off, and headed uphill on South Second Street, into the evening glow of another warm, but cloudy late spring day. It was supposed to rain later that night, which was much needed as the area hadn't seen much precipitation of late.

Denny ran and listened to Keith talk about how his outpatient therapy continued to progress, and all the writing he was continuing to do, lately focused on things from his childhood and growing up, trying to unlock certain memories which had been blocked out. Things about his parent's divorce, his Mom getting married shortly thereafter and moving to Indiana without even telling him or his two sisters. Having to always catch rides to school with some older kid in the neighborhood, who instead would drop him off like two miles outside of town, while he snuck into some older lady's house whose husband was at work. Bat shit crazy times that he didn't necessarily want to re-live or bring out into the light of the present day but was beginning to see the value in doing so. Since some of this repressed activity was acting upon his unconscious, helping to fuel the self-destructive behavior he had engaged in for some many years, like the proclivity to self-medicate with drugs or alcohol.

Keith said that he felt like he was slowly coming out of a mental fog he had been stuck in for longer than he could even recall. He was also being taught breathing techniques and mental exercises to cope with stressors when they did occur, which could keep him functioning fairly normally around his family and in the work environment, as well as any kind of social setting.

For now, his job seemed to be intact. The merger in the pipeline had been pushed back for at least another year, and perhaps it wouldn't even come to fruition at all, though Keith doubted that lady luck in the corporate world would be so kind. It would however, guarantee at minimum another year of steady work there, and after that it would come down to what departments were to be kept, and which were to be terminated locally. "Last week they let go of four programmers at the field office in King of Prussia. Told them they had a day to clear out and gave them two months' severance pay."

"Dam."

"I know one of the guys, Bill Boyer. Used to be in that fantasy football league we were in. Maybe you remember the name?"

"Sounds familiar. Liked the Browns?"

"Yes. That's him. From Ohio."

Keith and Denny slowly but steadily climbed up the familiar hills and into the heights. It seemed a little breezier up there and felt like it was going to start raining at any moment. Denny could tell Keith continued to get into better running shape, as he was able to take the hills with less effort; his breathing was not nearly as labored. "I can see what you tell me is true," Denny said.

"About the job?"

Denny laughed. "Well that too. I was referring to your running. I can see it's true that you have been getting out here quite regularly."

"Yes sir."

"I'm proud of you," Denny added, as they crested another hill and headed westward along the first ridgeline.

"Up in here is where I saw that bear the other night," Keith said as he pointed up ahead and to the left. "Came down out of the woods and right down to where the garbage cans were setting out. At the end of this driveway here."

"Guess it was hungry."

"Must have been." The two of them both started scanning the surroundings more intently for any sign of more bears. Though there wasn't any garbage scheduled to be picked up tomorrow, so no cans were out. "After all this it would have been a sick commentary on my life had it ended by being mauled by a bear while out running," Keith added, without a trace of self-pity in his voice.

"I would have felt partly responsible."

Dusk by now had settled upon the heights, beneath the puffy ceiling of cumulus clouds overhead, though there was still plenty of daylight left to complete the run. They did have the road to themselves as the two runners ran past a crumbling, old stone wall, which probably at one time helped form part of the property boundary to the Ukrainian Homestead. There was a dilapidated wooden barn on the far corner of the land, which looked like it would be blown to pieces the next time a strong thunderstorm rolled through, perhaps later tonight. Denny broke the temporary silence. "I've got some good news for you Keith."

"What?"

"You've been chosen to receive a free entry into the 2016 Richmond Marathon, to be held once again this coming November."

"Okay." Keith seemed nonplussed by the announcement, or more likely he didn't believe a word of what had just come forth from his friend's mouth. Which was understandable, considering Denny's penchant to delve into the depths of the absurd and senseless rather frequently.

"Will you accept such a stupendous, generous, and also may I add, potentially life changing gift?"

"Yes," he replied right off, "when you put it in such a context, I'd be a fool not too."

"That's the spirit and attitude being sought for this mighty endeavor. Happy to have you on board partner." And Denny went on to explain the whole operation to Keith, who was very intrigued by the idea once he confirmed that his buddy wasn't just yanking his chain, though he did hesitate somewhat to make a firm commitment as to the training that would be necessary to complete a marathon. But Denny was pretty confident that Keith would eventually commit to the entirety of the deal, even if it may require some more gentle prodding to be periodically applied on his part.

Denny also reminded his friend about how they used to have conversations about running marathons back in the day, although he didn't bring up about how they also used to talk about how cool it would be to qualify and run Boston. One step at a time, he prudently reasoned. And he himself had forgotten about all that heady talk too, until he got to thinking about the race, and thinking about asking Keith to run it with him. Who better to ask, after all this nightmarish ordeal he has been through, and was continuing to work his way out of?

"Wow. Twenty-six miles?"

"Twenty-six point two. Let us not discount that final point two my dear comrade."

"What have I gotten myself into," Keith groused with a sheepish grin on his face as they made the sharp right turn in the bottom of the hollow across from the Packerton Dam and headed up the monster known as Spring's Hill, the steepest of all the hills around.

Denny parked by the locks of the canal that he had run by so many times in the past few months. He crossed over the land bridge on foot then found the overgrown, thin trail that crashed through some thickets, and led out to the banks of the Lehigh River. He used a small flashlight to illuminate his way down the spooky pathway, though after a few minutes his eyes did adjust a little to the darkness.

He was leaving out in a few days, and Denny's heart seemed to weigh heavier inside as he crouched and listened to the sound of the waters flowing. The river itself was lower right now, and almost seemed to struggle to keep moving forward toward its destination; an almost hushed, warbling noise emanated from its mostly smooth surface. Denny put his hand in the water, which was fairly cold still despite all the warm weather of late. He tried not to think about Jennifer, though he couldn't fool himself, as he wished she was sitting there beside him. He would see her before hitting the road, something upon which they both agreed.

Denny tried to pray a little, but it was all sort of jumbled; his thoughts seemed to bounce arbitrarily about. He ruminated about his whole stay up there, and what if anything it had accomplished? Any lucid thoughts on the subject were not forthcoming tonight; the days, weeks, months had beat on, and that's how it all works, whether we are here in Pennsylvania, down in North Carolina, or any other place for that matter. And who takes measure of all such things anyhow? Denny didn't know. He always seemed to have an incessant yearning for more, an insatiable craving to go beyond what lie directly in front of him. That status quo failed at times to hold his interest, for it left him feeling restless, his compass askew.

Maybe he felt real alone, though he knew that wasn't really true. Yet in some ways he was. And in some ways, we ultimately are all alone. Perhaps that's why something deep inside of him craved those cosmic connections to that which was unseen-the uncreated light that he had recently read about. For then, perhaps, it made him feel a little more whole, a part of something much larger than himself, and less alone in all of it. There were always prices to be paid for our idiosyncratic tendencies. Denny picked up a rock and skipped it out across the water; it disappeared into the oily blackness of the river and of the night itself.

"I'm sure going to miss these dang breakfasts." Today it was the French Toast that seemed to melt inside one's mouth. Though the steak and cheese omelets were a close second as far as favorites for Denny.

"You were right about the French Toast. I feel like I'm in breakfast ecstasy right now," Jennifer said between bites.

One of the kitchen ladies, as Denny referred to the tender, affectionate women who worked in food preparations at the hotel, and seemed to look after him, came over to their table. He introduced Linda to Jennifer.

"Ahh," she smiled, "it's nice to finally meet you."

"This French Toast is to die for."

"Well thank Denny here for requesting a special order for today." She winked at him.

"I will. Nice meeting you," Jennifer replied.

The two of them filled themselves up on breakfast in the dining hall, and watched some families come and go and eat breakfast, before heading off for a day of whitewater rafting, hiking, or a wedding somewhere; several people were decked out in suits and dresses. Jennifer and Denny had stayed up half the night talking in his room, and once again felt it was best not to have any tearful goodbyes, or extended farewells, since that would merely exacerbate the situation. Simply put, it was what it was.

Denny told her about some lines he had read years ago in the liner notes of a Talking Head's CD. The lead singer David Byrne had written, "I hate goodbyes, I'd rather all of a sudden just not be there." He had always remembered that, since he had become fairly accustomed to being the one who had to leave.

Denny admitted to Jennifer that he had thought about proposing to her and asking her and her sons to move down to North Carolina with him; perhaps they could have purchased a little house in the countryside or something. And how he had even asked Trent where he should shop for a ring around here. But like they had discussed the one afternoon out on the trails, her and her family's life was here, and she couldn't fathom putting her boys through another major upheaval. And Jennifer said she could not stand the thought that if Denny moved back here, some part of him, no matter how small, might resent her for being the reason he had done so.

Before Jennifer got up to leave, Denny handed her a small black notebook, with a red ribbon tied around it. "Just a little something to remember me by, when we are separated by time and space."

"Oh Denny." She smiled as a tear rolled down her cheek. A few moments later she was gone; Denny wasn't sure if he'd ever see her again.

Before he hit the road, Denny decided to go visit the grave sites of his grandparents and mother, in their old church's cemetery that he hadn't set foot in since his Mom's funeral. It was a warm, sunny Sunday afternoon; he parked his car in a small parking lot across the street, and a little down from the road that led into the neighboring town's own municipal pool. When he got out of the car a strange sensation came over him, like deja vu. He looked back behind the trees, through which some abandoned tennis courts were visible, enclosed by metal fencing. As he stared at the unkempt courts, he remembered long forgotten memories from when he was young, very young. As a little child, maybe three, four years old, he had been brought there on church outings-one time he had tried to play tennis but had scuffed his older cousin's wooden racket on the court. And the pool; his Mom used to bring him there also when he was so very young, before he could even swim, or maybe even go into the water. There was some kind of summer camp in the park too. Denny stood there frozen, almost transfixed like he had seen a ghost, or several ghosts; he could almost see images of his mom and himself and others. They all looked so young, and happy. Music drifted down from up in the area of the pool, the kind of music that gets played where there are a lot of little kids around, like at a playground, or children's carnival.

Denny crossed the street and walked up one of the main walkways into the cemetery grounds, situated on several acres of a rolling, grassy hillside. He had a vague idea of where the headstones were; after meandering around for a few minutes he found all three of them grouped together. A small American flag stood next to his grandfather's tomb-he was a veteran of World War II. Denny sat down on the dry grass in front of the grave markers. He wished he had brought some flowers with, but the thought quickly passed. For how long he sat there he didn't know; it may have been five minutes, or thirty. On occasion when the wind would pick up, he would catch the faintest of sounds coming from the pool, including the music. Denny said a prayer for each of them, and bid farewell, not before promising that he would come back and visit again.

The last few days in Pennsylvania went by super quick. Denny got to see most everyone that he wanted to one last time before he headed out. Trent gave him an Army Track t-shirt, almost identical to the yellow ones they once had worn. "Wear it with pride," he said.

Denny photocopied two of the marathon training plans in the Pfzinger book and brought them over to a dinner he was invited to at the Druckenmillers the night before his departure. Keith was still a bit hesitant to undertake the challenge, though Denny assured him he could do it, and that he would coach him through it every step of the way. "May the road rise up to meet you," were Denny's last words, as he turned and walked down the cement walkway to his car. At the crack of the dawn the next morning, he was gone.

Chapter 11

When Denny returned to North Carolina the first thing he noticed was the humidity. And of-course it was hot, which was to be expected in June. But it was a noticeable contrast from the weather in Pennsylvania, where even on the days that were particularly warm, temperatures would drop off through the evening hours and overnight; there was a considerable less amount of moisture in the air. Not here. And he was back running in the flat lands. Denny quickly missed the contrasts in topography which the hills provided.

The short-term plan was to get a few runs in to re-acclimate to the heat and humidity, then compete in a 5k race being held in conjunction with the annual Blueberry Festival in the town of Burgaw, about thirty miles north of Wilmington. He had run this race a few years ago, and Denny wanted to see what kind of time he could lay down after all the training he had done. Bert had also commented that working on his "short game," as he termed it, would also prove to be beneficial when transitioning to marathon training, which would commence in a few weeks. In the interim, a reduction in mileage and intensity, would allow for some needed recovery from the winter and spring, and set him up for the increased demands which lie ahead. Denny knew more about training and racing shorter distances, so he was comfortable entrusting his friend to help guide his forthcoming ambitions.

"Well look what the cat dragged in?"

"Good to see you as well." Denny responded to Andrea, as he walked across the infield of the Ashley High School Track and Field complex. The Cape Fear Flyers were holding one of their last practices before the USATF North Carolina state meet held in Greensboro, on the famous blue track. "So how are we looking?"

"Not bad. But I assume though you've been checking the meet results on-line."

"Of course. I'll ride up to States."

"Awesome," she replied. "And we all missed you around here too."

That felt good to hear, as Denny walked around and said hi to several of the kids and fellow coaches. Jim instructed him they were doing a ladder workout tonight, 200s through 800s, and asked him if he wanted to jump in and pace some of the older boys.

"Sure thing."

"We don't pay people just to stand around. Coach 'em up son!" Denny spun around to greet Shane, who was carrying a clipboard in one hand, and had two stopwatches draped around his neck. Yes, Denny smiled inwardly, it was really good to be back. And once again, he got the intuitive feeling that he was right where he was supposed to be. The vision quest hadn't skipped a beat.

That Saturday Denny rode up to Burgaw with Xavier and Charlie through the early morning darkness. Gun time was set for 7am, in the theory that it would help the participants avoid at least a small measure of the day's heat. They hit the edge of a thunderstorm about half way through the forty-five-minute drive north, perhaps an ominous sign suggested Charlie, while Xavier added that if the sun comes out it will be like pea soup up there. Denny could do nothing but laugh. He wasn't in Kansas anymore.

The sun did come out, though fortunately it wasn't as blazing hot as perhaps it could have been, however the humidity levels were through the roof, nudging the heat index well into the eighties. Denny from his past knowledge recalled that the course was pancake flat but did have a fair amount of turns in it, and also one turnaround, though the last half mile was a straight shot in to the finish line.

A couple of fast runners he knew from Wilmington were there, which meant Denny had no chance of winning, or even getting on the podium. His goal was purely time oriented, and that was to break eighteen minutes. Which he did, with room to spare as he crossed the finish line in a time of 17:50, the fastest 5k Denny had run since his senior year on the cross-country team, and good enough for fifth place overall, and first place in the forty to forty-nine-year-old age group. Xavier took home third in the same age group, and Charlie captured the fifty to fifty-nine age group's top spot. Later, while eating a cone of homemade blueberry ice cream, Denny talked about how he was looking forward to some relaxed running and mileage coming up, though both his friends were skeptical that he'd be able to take his foot off the gas pedal.

The next couple of weeks though Denny was able to throttle back, while he rediscovered running the trails of the Carolina Beach State Park, located on the back side of the narrow island, and about a mile away from his condominium. He loved running on the network of trails there, which weren't too technical, and provided numerous spectacular views of the Atlantic Intracoastal Waterway, and the wide mouth of the Cape Fear River, as it flowed towards the Atlantic Ocean. Plus, he dug the sub-tropical vegetation growing like palmettoes and Venus fly traps and crossing through swampy marshes full of native wildlife such as hermit crabs, various snakes, and even the occasional alligator, as well as the large waterfowl which made their homes in there, such as herons and egrets. Though in the summer the park was full of mosquitos and horseflies, which were some of the nastiest insects Denny had ever encountered. Fortunately, they could usually be avoided if one stayed off the sandier trails back away from the water.

Some mornings an alarm was set real early and runs would occur while it was still dark out, usually to the north end of the island, which included about a half mile stretch of boardwalk right behind the dune lines. On such mornings Denny would listen to the surf coming onto the beach and catch sight of the white tops of the waves when they were two or three feet high. A few longer runs were also thrown in, on a southward route through Fort Fisher, a historic Civil War battle sight, and past the large aquarium complex located in the marshland near the southern end of the island.

After a short time, Denny adjusted back to the climate; just as cold weather and hills up north were encoded into his running DNA, a decade plus of running in the Carolinas had hardened him to the rigors of summertime running as well. He also started formulating plans for the upcoming cross-country season, realizing how eager he was to return to coaching on a regular basis.

Almost before Denny knew it; the time had arrived to begin the eighteen-week marathon training plan. Andrea had also put together some shorter circuit workouts for him to work the upper body and core, as well as the legs. The Pfzinger plan he had chosen started off with weekly mileage totals in the low to mid-sixties, with a long run of fifteen to seventeen miles in length. Eventually the mileage would top out at seventy-five to eighty miles per week and consisted of a steady diet of mid-week medium long runs in the twelve to fifteen-mile range, sometimes even on back to back days, in addition to the weekly long runs on Sundays. Bert had told him those mid-week medium-long runs runs were the types of workouts often overlooked in marathon training, as most people tended to focus solely on that one long run per week, usually done on a Saturday or Sunday.

In the first mesocycle, there was also a weekly threshold run, and general aerobic runs with sets of hundred-meter striders. Denny could see this was going to be a challenging slog, which Bert had forewarned him of as well. He had never done that much long running before, especially not multiple times per week. Yes, this was going to likely take him places physiologically, and spiritually, where he had yet to set foot; exactly what he desired. Denny suspected he was going to get a good taste of where some of those invisible boundaries that he liked to write and talk about were in fact located, and that a high degree of fortitude and resolve would be necessary if he were to see his way to whatever might lie on the other side. Maybe this was all just the beginning of it he mused, even though he was hard pressed to define once again, just what it was that he sought. Denny began to write a letter to Jennifer about how this all might allow him to continue to scale the ladder into some unknown fourth dimension, but he crumpled the piece of notebook paper up and tossed it in the waste bin.

Later into the hot, long summer, Denny met Bert early one Sunday morning for an eighteen-mile run. It was still pretty dark outside as the silhouette of a runner coming up Hamlet

Street approached Denny. Bert always ran with such an economical, effortless stride; his five-foot ten-inch muscular frame exhibited nary an inch of wasted motion, as he fully emerged into view. Which always made Denny a tad jealous, since he himself didn't have the smoothest of running forms. Bert had also grown a full, reddish brown beard since he had last seen him, and was dressed in a tank top and trucker type baseball cap on his head. Denny was shirtless as usual, which would likely last well into September.

"How's it going brother?"

"I'm blessed my friend," Denny replied. "Nice to see you again."

The two runners weaved through the small, deserted downtown area of Carolina Beach and up onto the boardwalk. A young man was fast asleep on one of the swinging benches that faced the ocean. "Must have been a good night," Bert remarked. The Atlantic was barely visible, though the sound of its waves was audible which Denny listened to, along with the sound of their shoes hitting the wooden boards. Way out on the horizon the palest trace of bluish light was also visible, where the sea met the sky. Several sea gulls stirred on the beach; laughing gulls with their eponymous calls. The light on-shore breeze felt pleasant on Denny's exposed body, and it wasn't all that hot yet, though certainly fairly humid. The slight smell of salt water wafted up onto the boardwalk. Denny once had a friend who was a reiki; she had told him about the medicinal powers inherent in the air by the ocean, and all the benefits one could obtain just through absorption. It had something to do with all the iodine in salt water.

They ran up Canal Street for two miles to the end of town, then cut under a long fishing pier attached to an old wooden house that had been converted into a tackle shop and bar. Past the pier, the two of them headed onto the beach, where the sand was always hard packed and much easier to run on, unlike most areas which Denny detested, and almost always avoided. But the north end of the island was much different and was also uninhabited; the only way to access was with a four-wheel drive vehicle, or via the old shoe leather express.

The sun began to poke the top part of its head up, way off and out to the east, and above the now visible demarcation where the ocean met the sky. Pretty soon it looked like a fiery, reddish orange beach ball emerging out of the panoramic sweep of the Atlantic's endless waters. The sun cast beams of light that skittered off the waves as they rose upward, then hung suspended in midflight for a fraction of a second, before plunging back downward into where they had come from, throwing a foamy spray towards the shoreline. "So beautiful," Denny remarked, rather devoutly to Bert.

"We do live in our own little slice of nirvana, don't we?"

"Amen."

Both the runners said little more as they rounded the bend near the far northern tip of the island, where a shallow channel of water served to partition the land they ran on with a smaller, completely uninhabited island. Hundreds and hundreds of gulls and other shore birds were gathered there, feeding in the early morning light. A few people were fishing there as well, casting lines well out into the gently rollicking waters.

Later in the run, after the sun was out in full force and the temperatures began to climb, Bert and Denny made their way into the Carolina Beach State Park for the remaining six to seven miles of the workout. The shelter of the woods provided some relief from the heat, and there were many places to obtain drinking water, including several old-fashioned hand crank pumps in the campgrounds. Denny hated to carry his own water. He had tried using hand held bottles, a belt with smaller attached bottles, and even a hydration vest, but would always end up shucking whatever he had a mile or two into the run, choosing comfort over any immediate hydration needs, preferring ultimately to rely on finding his own sources of water.

Bert had a sixteen-ounce hand held bottle attached with a Velcro strap to his one hand, and would periodically take sips from, and also offer Denny drinks too, which he would politely decline. But once into the park, Denny steered the run towards the closest fountain. He knew, or thought he knew, where just about every public source of water was on the entire island, including sinks in bathrooms, and hose nozzles on the sides of community buildings like churches. "You should map it online," Bert suggested.

"Yeah. Good idea," Denny agreed as he cranked the handle of one of the pumps up and down a few times until water began to flow out of its head. He cupped his hands beneath and took a couple good drinks. "Invaluable information for stubborn, picky runners like me," he added.

The park and its trails were home to Bert as well; it was actually where the two of them had first met many years ago, on one of the big informal group runs that Shane used to organize on the weekends. "Remember when we used to follow the unmarked trails all the way down to behind the National Guard housing?"

"Yes. I miss that. Even more wild than in here," Denny replied as they made their way along a rather narrow single-track trail situated at the edge of the woods, and smack up against about a thirty-foot sand embankment parallel to the Atlantic Intracoastal Waterway. Several years ago, the Army had begun to crackdown on trespassing on huge swaths of the island's backside, or west side, which also contained a labyrinth of trails, some of which dated back to the Civil War. And these trails went for miles; one of them even cut right by the abandoned ruins of the Dow Chemical plant, which was rumored to have made poisonous gasses used during World War II. One time a few of them had found some kind of underground cement bunker, with old rusted metal hooks hanging from the ceiling. Perhaps it used to be a secret torture chamber where these gasses were tested, one of the runners in all seriousness, had hypothesized.

Bert asked him how the training was going so far, and the specifics of which plan he was following, and how he felt like he was handling or reacting to the workload so far. Denny broke it down for him, as well as some of the running and training he had previously done, and how it all compared. The mileage he was handling okay, but he struggled trying to maintain paces, especially on the threshold runs. "The other day I was supposed to do five miles at LT pace, as part of a nine-mile run. I ran down Lake Park Boulevard to about the aquarium, then turned around to put the hammer down on the way back. I got into the second mile and I couldn't even come close to holding a 6:20 pace. Hell, I could barely maintain marathon pace."

"That'll happen," Bert said with an air of knowledge that put Denny at ease. "Especially in this heat and humidity. Also, the accumulated fatigue of the long runs and mileage can get to you. Just do what you can pace wise on those days, but get the miles in."

"Yes, I did do the ten."

"Good. Key is not to panic. And to stick with it. There will always be some rougher patches."

They picked up Sugar Loaf Trail, which was wider and easier to run on, and looped the perimeter of the park on the west and south sides. Bert caught Denny up on how his two daughters Sophia and Sydney were doing, and about his new job doing geological research at the university. And how his wife Anslee, whom Denny also knew and was friends with, was thinking about doing another triathlon in the fall. "It's tough for both of us to train for something big at the same time. So, since I did Boston, it's her turn in the fall."

"Makes sense."

Denny also compared some of the trails he had run in Pennsylvania with the trails in the state park. And how different it had been to run hills again, and in cold weather. "It's funny. I had some runs where I was so cold. And you try of course to take your mind off it or trick yourself. Think about warmth, the sun, right? Picture how these warm weather runs would feel again, like out here with no shirt on. Then it's so freaking hot like this, so I start to remember all those colder runs, wearing long sleeves, gloves, looking at snow."

Bert laughed. "We are never satisfied."

"It gives us something to rally against I guess."

But they survived, and got over eighteen miles in, in a little over two hours and forty minutes. Which capped the week off for Denny at seventy-three-miles. He was feeling lean and hungry, as the sweat poured down off him and dropped to the ground. Though he knew he had much, much more left on the docket, and many more long runs to get through, as he slowly climbed the four flights of wooden stairs up to his condo, and the cooler air contained within. Once inside he got right into his post run strength and mobility exercises, practicing what he had recently read in a Jay Johnson article about the importance of doing, even after long runs. There was a text message from Keith: "15 miles longest run yet was a bit of a struggle. 14 weeks and counting to Richmond hope I be ready."

"Trust the process," Denny replied.

Many nights after he had finished dinner, and about the time darkness had fully wrapped herself around the island, Denny liked to walk over to the beach and sit by the ocean. This particular evening, he made himself a cup of lemon wheatgrass tea, added two teaspoons of honey, then carefully poured the mug of hot liquid into a thermos before heading out the door. Once on the sands of the beach, Denny headed south, away from the more lit up center part of town, until he found a nice quiet spot to sit down at. He took off an old pair of running shoes he had on, and stretched his muscular, tan legs in the warm sand, then laid down on his back. The sky was pin pricked with swarms of stars swirled all about. One very bright star stood out, which was actually the planet Mars, or so Denny thought.

The waves of the ocean came in rather gentle and benign this evening; small rollers which broke just off shore, and meekly sent shallow pools of water onto the sand, losing their meager momentum a few feet up the beach, before receding back into the sea. The moon was perhaps ninety percent full; it hung suspended in the sky well out over the ocean, and cast a pale-yellow light down onto the smooth, glassy surface of the water in an inverted 'V' like shape, similar to the outline that a flock of migrating geese made. The tea had a sharp, distinct lemony flavor; "very fine," Denny said quietly, as if to not disturb the tranquility of the scene.

Sometimes Denny would try to allow his mind to go blank, such as the attempts at meditation he would make while sitting up in the cold and the snow of Pennsylvania. Here, though, he would stare out at the ocean; the sight and sound of the waves could put him into some sort of semi-hypnotic trance. Denny would keenly stare at spots in the water where he thought a wave might break from, and then on the occasions when he could start to see the white foaminess on the developing wave's crest, it would temporarily dazzle him, as if the wave itself had been willed by his own imagination. Or Denny would close his eyes for a short time; then when he opened them and was looking once again out at the ocean, all of it seemed fresh and newly discovered, as if he was first beholding the beauty and raw power of nature herself. He would pray too, nothing in particular usually, but just allow his heart to be open and accept God's grace, like he was reading about again in a Saint Francis de Sales book.

Tonight, he thought about Jennifer. He wondered what she was up to at that very moment and wished like mad that he could show her all of this right here, right now. Maybe she was outside too, looking up at the same moon and the stars that he was? Or down in the basement painting, caught up in one of her own ecstatic frenzies. Did she miss him too? Did she wonder if they had made a mistake as well? Maybe though she didn't think about it much at all, but he suspected in his heart of hearts that wasn't the case. Denny swore he could feel the soft touch of her hand running through his shaggy hair, but he knew it was just the breeze coming off the ocean. Still, it was fun to pretend. They had agreed it was for the best and agreed not to talk for a while. She had kids to raise; he had truths to chase-

Denny hadn't even realized that he was gently weeping, a lone man sitting in solitude on the infinite sands of his beach, while the world continued to spin on its invisible axis, propelling the long, dark night on towards the light of yet another tomorrow.

Chapter 12

The dog days of August found Denny dog tired after many a run; he was headlong into the teeth of his marathon training plan. Bert had told him that there would be times when each runner had to answer for his or her self how badly they wanted it, and that there was a reason qualifying for Boston wasn't an easy thing to do. Denny swore he could taste the salt from his sweat, as he watched it stream in bubbly white rivulets down his legs halfway into most runs. Andrea suggested dietary additions to his nutrition like celery and red beets which both helped to absorb water, that in turn would help to maintain hydration levels. The miles added up week after week; the midweek long runs were up to fifteen miles on select days, and again there were those back to back ones of say twelve miles on a Tuesday, followed by fourteen on a Wednesday. Denny feared to look ahead to the next day, or the next week, and was convinced this Pfzinger character was a diabolical masochist.

On one particular warm, humid evening, as he slogged through a grueling fourteen-miler, Denny thought anyone can sit at a desk and type numbers into boxes, right? God I'm losing it Denny admitted, as his socks began to squish inside his running shoes on yet another run. He decided to duck into a newer extension of the state park called the Fitness Trail, a mile loop made of dirt and gravel that wound its way through a wooded tract of land across the street from the main entrance. Last fall Denny had helped out on a community volunteer project to lay all the dirt in there, on top of black plastic that was initially used to demarcate the trail. There were fitness stations scattered about the loop; contraptions with bars that could be used to do chin-ups, or crunches, or small structures with spinning wheels that probably could be used for some kind of upper body workout.

Denny reasoned he could go in there and tick some of the remaining miles off one at a time; that somehow from a mental standpoint this would make the task a little more digestible, or doable. But after two laps he had had enough of all that, plus he needed more water, so he headed on out and back into the state park to the visitor's center, and the closest source of water. Once there, at the precious water fountain outside of the bathrooms, Denny allowed himself a few moments to stop and slowly walk after taking a drink of cold water, before hitting the start button again on his watch, and plunging into the woods onto one of the trails.

He felt like he was on his own version of a death march, with an ungodly six and a half miles still left to be done. At that point he did not care in the least anymore about pace, or even stopping again for a few moments to walk; no, the sole objective had devolved into simply hitting the target mileage, no matter how ugly it all got. He came back around to the visitor's center for another drink and another short rest, and since it had become just about too dark to safely see the trails, Denny headed up to what was called the Greenway, a macadam bike path about a half mile long, adjacent to the front boundary of the park.

It was pretty dark there, and no-one else at the moment could be seen, so Denny decided to take off his shorts and just run in his boxers, as a means of shedding some weight, since what limited clothing he had on was all thoroughly drenched with sweat. So, he ran back and forth on the Greenway several times in his boxers, something he had never done, nor ever imagined he would ever do. Denny's brain was perhaps as soaked as his body, but he was beyond caring at that juncture in the run what anyone might think, as he clung to the sound of Bert's voice repeating over and over again, "how bad do you want this?"

A week and a half later from his short-less ramble, twenty-one miles was on the agenda. Denny began by first running to the north end of the island and back, then crossed Snow's Cut Bridge, which spanned the Atlantic Intracoastal Waterway, and headed up Carolina Beach Road, the main thoroughfare off the island to Wilmington. The first five miles or so on Carolina Beach Road were slightly uphill, until he turned left onto Cathay Road, and into a neighborhood named Monterey Heights, which perhaps unfairly had the reputation of being sort of a poor white trash area, at least in contrast to some of the more opulent affluence located nearby. This always amused Denny, not that he really knew why, though he did feel more at home running thru "the Heights." He stopped first and used the hose attached to a faucet located on the side of one of the gas stations on the corner. Denny also had a Clif Bar in his pocket but was experimenting doing all his long runs without ingesting any calories, therefor training his body to predominately use its own fat stores as fuel, which he had read about in the *Advanced Marathoning* book.

A solid chunk of the back half of the run was on River Road, which took its name from the Cape Fear River, that was just off to the west. Denny could distract himself by looking across the marshes at the wide flowing river; today a large barge ship was making its way north, most likely headed for the major port located just before Wilmington, about ten miles upriver. And the miles were clicking off with fluid precision, one after the other, which pleased Denny that he was running this workout without much strain, hitting most of the mile splits in the low eight-minute range, right about what he wanted to be doing. The accumulation of mileage was perhaps beginning to bear fruit; the Sunday long runs weren't quite as daunting of a specter both physically and mentally, as he was becoming a bit more calloused to the potpourri of physiological factors at play, some of which undoubtedly existed beneath the realm of consciousness.

He finished the run strong, worn out a little which was to be expected, but strong nonetheless. The average mile pace ended up being 8:03, and Denny knew that he had more left in the tank. The math Denny had already computed beforehand, but now that he had successfully completed the run, he allowed himself the pleasure of re-calculating the week's final tally; today's twenty-one miles, added to the mileage of the past six days, put the total for the week at seventy-eight miles, his highest to date, and fourth week in a row in the seventies.

One night as Denny meandered along the beach, he pondered over something he had recently read about people who suffer from eating disorders, more specifically in regards to young women. That the act of eating and making oneself purge, or not eating at all, essentially what a person did to their own body, was something that they felt like they could control. And it was likely the only thing of which they felt they had any control over, in a world around them which seemed hostile in its multitudinous pressures brought to bear, most of which could not be controlled. Therefore, what went in, or did not go into their bodies, assumed an unhealthy, paramount importance in their minds, regardless of the detrimental, and sometimes catastrophic consequences of said behaviors.

Denny, who had lived for many years under the dual lashes of drugs and alcohol, certainly understood what it was like to feel the illusion of control over that which was in actuality, controlling oneself. But in an ironic, twisted sort of way, he wondered if just perhaps, he was engaged in a similar psychological behavioral pattern with his own running? He subjected himself to intense rigors almost to the point of flogging himself at times, because it was an activity he was in control of; the master of his own destiny in such pursuits, cloaked under the guise of intense training. Denny wasn't quite sure if all of this did add up, as he gazed way up ahead at the string of tiny lights illuminating the Kure Beach fishing pier, two miles away. He did dismiss it as a bit of malarkey, though the subject wasn't entirely forgotten, and could be chalked up to perhaps another glimpse behind the veil, albeit something he didn't want to necessarily see. In the end though, these things always ended up fascinating Denny; he had lost most any fear of going down dark alleyways in his mind a long time ago.

Meanwhile Denny was more actively preparing to coach another Cross-Country season; XC, or Cross as he liked to refer to it as. First practice would be in less than two weeks; he had lined up a staff, most of them were returning coaches and friends. He had also gotten approval from the organization's Board of Directors for all the dates and times needed for practices and meets, as well as some monetary allocations for things like uniforms and travel costs and made sure all the paperwork was updated and on-file with USATF. It was a labor of love for Denny, as he took out a yellow note pad and started to sketch out a generalized workout plan for the season. He had a good idea of the composition of the roster and was excited to have an excellent crop of middle school boys returning to run.

It was a time of the year he thoroughly enjoyed. Denny had learned over the years that summers in the South tended to beat one into a pulp; it was a challenge to endure their length and severity, such as the case could be made for winters in the North. But the first signs of fall weren't too far around the corner now, as the last days of August slipped on by. Runners in the community were talking more about what bigger races they were going to focus on in the fall season, such as Charlie and fellow coach Jim who were going to run the Battleship Half Marathon in Wilmington. Several members of the Wilmington Road Runners Club were training for the Marine Corps Marathon, and a few were headed to Chicago for that city's annual October twenty-six-point two-mile race. There was also a full menu of shorter races locally as well.

The following Sunday Denny had nineteen miles, with ten miles at goal marathon pace, on the schedule. Fortunately, it was not quite as warm when he began the run a little before six am. His target marathon finishing time was three hours and ten minutes, which would put him five minutes under the time needed to qualify for Boston, more than enough he was told by several runners to almost assuredly be accepted into the field. Plus, the time had this mythical resonance in his family's history, as tattered as it might be in this present day and age. The pace needed was right around 7:15 per mile, which Denny planned to run today. First, he ran four miles on the island, then headed on up towards Snow's Cut Bridge, and to the same route he had been incorporating into all of his long runs, which was about a fifteen-mile loop.

Denny completed the first nine miles rather easily in the low to mid eights, using those early miles to sort of wake the body and mind up to the task at hand. Sometimes the first few miles were actually the toughest for him mentally, since when at say the three or four-mile mark, Denny was painfully aware of how many more miles still had to be run, despite the fact that physically, running a few miles well over an eight minute per mile pace was like a walk in the park these day. But once he had knocked out all of the first nine miles, Denny sought to groove and settle into a much faster pace, which he hoped to maintain for the remaining distance left in the workout.

He checked his watch periodically, especially early on to try and be as accurate as he could be dialing in the preferred pace. Then, if warranted, corrections could be made, either by picking the pace up say a half click or slowing it down by some similar margin. Denny went through the first pace-mile in 7:17, right about where he wanted to start out; he knew it might require him a mile or two to settle into the running rhythm he sought. During the second mile he only glanced at his watch twice and went through the mark in 7:14. Excellent he thought, based on the perceived effort he was exerting, coupled with the fact that he had been running into a bit of a westerly head wind for most of that mile. Headed down River Road, back towards the island, the third mile was done in 7:12; and the subsequent remainder of the run went very well, as Denny pretty much maintained a pace within five to ten seconds of the target, while getting to experience and battle through some fatigue in his legs and upper body the last several miles. He even slowed the pace down twice during the final three miles, a positive marker. Denny had enjoyed the views of the ocean and waterway atop the bridge, and the hill on its ascent hadn't affected him much. All told, things were humming along nicely; his mileage total for the week was seventy-six miles, and a recovery week was upcoming as well.

Which was appreciated and much needed, though Denny was reluctant to ease up on the training. Though he could step back, and with a rational mind assess his progress within the overall context of the plan and see how a periodic reduction in mileage every several weeks was a beneficial thing. His mindset had evolved, as he now had become wired into the challenge of looking ahead at the daily runs and workouts and figuring out how to bring it all to fruition, within the scope of all the other activities that lie ahead such as employment, and coaching obligations. To borrow the words from a playwright, who's name escaped him, when asked why he did what he did, had answered, "I can't not do it." Denny continued to fuel the tempest inside, while learning to function, and even thrive within the turbulence it created. He had gotten to a point where he too, couldn't not do it. In the chosen voyage Denny stayed out to sea, eschewing any safe port; when Celine asked him to elucidate further, the best he could say was that he was finding it more and more impossible to live some kind of a staid existence.

"Yes. I understand," she said. Celine picked up a big coffee mug with two hands and took a sip, then looked at Denny from above the rim and added, "but I am whack job too."

"We pay our own bills," he responded, with the sense of conviction of one who believes in the veracity of the road being travelled.

"No one can ever accuse us of being dull." And that was the truth. She had survived her own wrecking ball too and had come out the other side and grew into one of the feistiest, most energetic people he had ever known, with big brown eyes that had the habit of almost bulging out of their sockets when she became animated.

"Screw the bastards if they don't understand. We aren't out to harm anyone. And good things can come out of what we are trying to do." Celine wrote for several blogs that tackled the subjects of abuse and neglect in the long-term health care system for the elderly; her and a colleague had recently published a book of anecdotes from their years working in medical facilities.

She had been encouraging her friend Denny for years to "get it all down on paper," which he was finally in the process of attempting. And that if nothing else, it was fun to create, through his own written words, another perhaps parallel world that he could vicariously live in. But he had his doubts and wasn't so sure where the whole project was heading. Celine had volunteered to read some of it, and said it was riveting material, though he suspected she was just being a little too kind. Nonetheless he appreciated the input. Before they left the coffeehouse, Celine gave Denny a little piece of paper that was folded up several times into a little triangle. "Look at this tonight before you go to sleep. And anytime you feel you need a little inspiration."

"I most certainly will. Thank you."

And not to be one to mess with such explicitly stated directions, Denny waited until later that night to unfold the paper to get at its mysterious contents. It was one big paragraph hand written in neat, but very tiny printed block letters which read:

"If you are going to try, go all the way. Otherwise don't even start. This could mean losing girlfriends, wives, relatives and maybe even your mind. It could mean not eating for three or four days. It could mean freezing on a park bench. It could mean jail. It could mean derision. It could mean mockery-isolation. Isolation is the gift. All others are a test of your endurance, how much you really want to do it. And you'll do it, despite rejection and the worst odds. And it will be better than anything else you can imagine. If you're going to try, go all the way. There is no other feeling like that. You will be alone with the gods, and the night will flame with fire. You will ride life straight to perfect laughter. It's the only good fight there is." - Charles Bukowski.

Denny tacked the note up beside his bed and went to sleep.

The recovery week went well, though Denny had to laugh when he told Bert that he never imagined he'd run sixty-one miles in a week and call it recovery.

"You're getting it brother," was his reply.

Denny was getting it. He was getting it and getting after it with the zealousness of a religious convert being indoctrinated into the church of high mileage. Sure, there were the attendant minor aches and pains; his left Achilles tendon had been fairly sore for the past few days, and it was still a bit tender to the touch. His right knee, the front part sort of under the knee cap felt a bit funny sometimes on runs, as if something might be moving around inside there, though it did not cause him any pain. Jim suggested it might be loose cartilage.

After the first workout of shorter repetitions at 5k pace, which was six times 800 meters, Denny's hamstrings were tender and fairly sore. But he knew all that was to be expected, and like any runner, he knocked on wood that no serious injury would rear its ugly head and cause him to miss any extended training time. Denny also had to learn to deal with some moodiness, or mood swings, which in his case manifested themselves in a shorter temper, or impatience with inanimate objects like electronics. Once he even hit the base of his laptop when the internet was frozen and stuck loading a page; ironically a website with results from a race that Suzanne and Carla had run in up in Pennsylvania. At first Denny thought he had broken the whole computer but was relieved when he realized he had just knocked the power out, though it was a cause for him to step back and sort of have a little come to Jesus moment with himself.

Andrea told him that excessive exercise could cause hormonal imbalances, and to also make sure he was getting enough sleep at night. Perhaps he was in some sort of a state of evolving, like caterpillars into butterflies? There had to be a little pain and discomfort in that, he told Celine.

"Keep at it cowboy," was her response.

Which Denny did, knocking out his first eighty-mile week, that culminated with a twenty-two-mile run on Sunday morning.

The following evening was the Flyer's first Cross Country practice of the fall. Once again, the club would be practicing at Veteran's Park, an outdoor complex of soccer and baseball fields with open, green spaces in between, located on a sprawling school grounds which included the Ashley High School football field and track stadium, that they would use as well. Denny arrived there after work, and then ran an easy three miles pretty much around the perimeter. Over the past few years he had become so intimately familiar with the place, that him and others simply referred to it as campus. It was another running home to him; the sights and sounds washed back over him as he ran by the football team practicing on the field behind the stadium, and the cheer squad and band assembled in front of the high school. Indeed, it was that time of the year again.

Fifty-eight kids had signed up, ranging in age from seven to seventeen, most of whom were gathered near a picnic shelter dubbed home base for most of the season. Denny was attired in one of his green and gold coaches' t-shirts, had a whistle around his neck, and clipboard in hand. He blew the whistle and called everyone over to sit down on the grass before the team began their warm-up run and drills. Once he had everyone's attention, no small feat in and of itself, he started with some brief remarks he had prepared, aware that the collective attention span of such a group was quite limited.

First though, he introduced himself and the other coaches, and had each kid stand up and say their name as well, before getting into the heart of some of what he hoped to impart upon the young harriers throughout the upcoming campaign.

"Ladies. Gentleman. We ask two things of you at each practice." Denny roamed back and forth as he spoke, trying to make eye contact with as many kids as possible. "One-that you have a positive attitude and try your best. This means coming out here even after a bad day at school, when you missed some answers on a test, or your best friend decided not to sit with you at lunch. You come out here and forget about that and focus on what we are going to do here. Always think in terms of what you can do, not what you can't do. For instance, instead of saying I can't run three miles without walking, say I can run one mile, or run two miles without stopping." Denny sensed some fidgeting, that his time was about to run out fast. "And number two. This is real important. So please listen to this. Let's all have fffuunnnnnn!" With that, he did elicit a modest response from the charges, as they got up and followed him and Andrea on a half mile warm up loop around the soccer fields.

"Way to motivate the troops coach," she said to him as they slowly jogged. "We are going to have quite the year!"

Denny wasn't sure just how much dead pan was in her remarks, but it was nice to have her around, and the other coaches and kids for another season of cross.

He still thought a lot about Jennifer; they hadn't spoken, written to each other, texted-nothing since he had left out of Pennsylvania, though the two of them had talked at length a few times about giving each other space once they'd be physically apart. This is silly, Denny thought as he paced around the small living room in his condominium, or as he sat on the back porch and looked over at the ocean, partially visible between two hotel buildings. At the beach itself he'd scan the skies for another shooting star, so he could make another feeble wish, though for what specifically, he did not know. One evening at practice he even got into a conversation about her with Otto, his top runner and an eighth grader in school, as he was in the middle of running a workout of 300-meter repeats at mile race pace. "Sounds like. She could be. The one. Coach," he offered.

Denny wrote a long letter but did not send it. For it wouldn't have accomplished anything he rationalized, in the same vein of rationalization he engaged in as to why he didn't want to contact her before she did him. One lonely fool, arguing with himself he thought, as he turned to prayer for guidance. Charlie gave him a copy of a book called the *Ragamuffin Gospel,* by Brennan Manning after they met up one Saturday for a run in the state park. He told Denny that he had read it a few times, and it had helped him when he was having trouble with a similar travail in his own life.

The temperatures continued to cool some, and the incessantly high humidity levels diminished a little as the month of September seemed to fly by. Denny would go one evening a week to the farm to run his scheduled interval workouts, which had replaced the weekly threshold runs in the plan. It wasn't actually a farm; Denny wasn't quite sure why he had named the series of dirt roads that connected large drainage ponds behind several housing developments in the middle part of the island as such, though he did often see wild animals there like white-tailed deer, and numerous species of birds. And about an eight-foot alligator made its home in one of the ponds. The beauty though of the farm was that it was isolated, and free from vehicular traffic, and had a nice softer, yet fast surface to run on.

On tap this particular go-around was five by 1200 meters at five-kilometer pace, with 400-meter recovery jogs. Denny knew that this one would be grueling, since he'd be doing 6,000 meters worth of running at a pace which in theory, could only be maintained for 5,000 meters. Though the recovery jogs made it possible to complete the workout. After a twenty-minute warm-up run he was off and blazing around the edge of one of the drainage ponds. A lone egret watched him run.

Denny checked his pace every so often, as he rounded up onto another dirt road which bisected a wooded area, that also served to keep the stretch of terrain predominately in the shade. The hard-packed dirt felt much better on his legs, then all the asphalt he had been doing most of his running on of late. He was trying to keep the pace at about 5:50, which would equate to a 1200-meter time close to four minutes and fifteen seconds. He finished the first in 4:14, and the second one was right about where he wanted it to be as well, which included having to slow down to go around two yellow metal gates on either side of Ocean Boulevard, the one actual road he did have to cross, in order to connect up the two sections of the farm.

The large water tower stood just up ahead by the time Denny commenced repetition number three, and by now a reasonable amount of lactic acid had accumulated in his legs. He broke the segment up into thirds, focusing on getting through a quarter mile at a time; sort of a mental aide in staving off the insidious physical creep of the waste fluid inside his lower extremities, that would continue to render his two legs progressively heavier as he covered more ground. Denny was gassed and about out of breath as he finished number three and eased into a very slow jog with his hands on his hips, and head titled slightly backwards. Several strides later he took his right hand off his hip and flashed three fingers in the air, his own peculiar way of marking off the progress being made. "Get me through the next one God. Please," he pleaded, just before he took off on number four.

And that quickly Denny was into the oncoming torrent, the waiting flood. He tried on certain reps to hold back a little, or to run slightly above pace for maybe the first quarter mile, especially on the latter ones to forestall the lactic acid drip until as late as possible. Then he would pick up the tempo, trying to finish real hard in say the last two to three hundred meters to ameliorate the time difference, though his usual practice was to run them consistently throughout.

A glance at his watch three tenths of a mile in, revealed that a miscalculation had occurred; the pace read 5:25. But Denny stayed with it, as best as he could, grinding hard in the last part and finishing in 4:03. He dry-heaved twice too in the last hundred meters, and then sort of stumbled into the recovery jog; initially slower than a walk. Denny's fingers dug into the flesh just above his hips, though after a short bit some feeling returned to his enervated legs, and his breathing lost its spasmodic tenor, enough so that he flashed four fingers and looked up at the dirt road ahead, while asking God for just one more. Number five he diligently knocked out, just as he had knocked out the previous four. Once again, he dry-heaved, a little before the conclusion of the repetition, but then it was all over.

And when it was all over a primordial silence filled his head and seemed to send an invisible golden wave on down throughout his body, as if he had fallen into a meditative, hallowed trance. Denny almost lost track of where he was, or who he was-the splash of colors in the late evening sky captivated him, as he slowly ran on back home.

When he got back home and checked his cell phone he saw he had missed two calls from Keith and had received a text from his well that read, "call me when you get this." Well this can't be good, Denny thought, as he called back. Suzanne answered, which immediately confirmed his suspicions. She explained that Keith was okay, but that he had been checked back into the hospital for a few days, as apparently, he had stopped taking some of the prescribed medications he was still on and had some kind of episode at work. Which as much as she had been able to glean was that he had threatened to burn the place down if upper management didn't disclose exactly when the realignment plans would be implemented, and when the merger was to occur.

"Jesus," was the only thing Denny could think of to say.

And to show how serious Keith was, he had borrowed a lighter from a coworker who smoked and was attempting to light the contents of a waste basket on fire when he was physically restrained by two security guards, and summarily escorted out of the building and off the premises. "My guess is that'll be end of his career there," Suzanne added.

"Anything I can do from here?"

"He's stable now and should be out in a few days and seems to be quite aware that he needs to stay on the medical regiment. And also, that an update to the resume is needed." Denny thought he could hear a shade of amusement in Sue's voice when she said the last part about the resume. Maybe it wasn't so bad after all, and Keith had gotten the clean break he needed, though through a less than ideal means. Hopefully there wouldn't be any legal charges.

“Hey," he added, before the call ended, "I didn't get all straightened out the first time around either. Sometimes it takes what it takes."

"That's what I've been told. How's your training going? Keith has been telling me a few things."

"Good thanks. Just ran some 1200s tonight. Hurt a wee bit," he said.

"I don't know how you handle all that on top of all the miles."

"I'm not always quite sure myself."

After they said goodbye, Denny tossed the phone onto his futon couch and mulled back over a few things. Keith had texted him just the other day, Monday if memory served, which was three days ago. He had told him how good he had felt on his runs and how he was getting his confidence back after some longer runs cut short. And how he was finally becoming convinced and confident that he could finish the dang thing, hopefully without walking too. Who knows, thought Denny, all of us are pretty adept at donning a certain veneer, even to those who are closest to us. They were a little more than seven weeks out from the race; Denny hoped that this setback would not derail his friend's rendezvous with the big twenty-six-point-two.

After a dinner of scrambled eggs, leftover chicken, and brown rice mixed into burritos, Denny walked over to the beach. The surf rolled in, sending four to five-foot-high waves crashing down into the ocean, before shooting water well up onto the sand. There was a category two hurricane well off the coast towards the south and east, but some of its peripheral effects were evident all the way up here, hundreds of miles away. Denny was always respectfully in awe of the sheer power and reach of such weather systems. It was dark on the beach; the moon and stars obscured by a high layer of cirrus clouds. A light, but steady breeze blew, which felt warm and real humid; it scattered sea foam up and down the beach near the waterline.

Denny reached his right hand inside his short's pocket and fumbled with his cell phone before pulling it out and illuminating it to see, but then he put it back inside the same pocket again. Why this should be so difficult, and why he should feel such a panicky like quivering sensation in his body, he did not know? So, Denny sat down and absentmindedly watched the ocean for a short while, as wave after wave rose up out of the churned-up waters, and noisily plummeted back into the ocean, time and time again.

Finally, he reached into his pocket again and pulled the phone out, found the stored name and hit the call button, before there was any chance to reconsider. As the phone began dialing, and he could hear the electronic ringing sounds being made, Denny swore that his heart was about to leap out of his chest. He took some deep, short breaths to steady himself, as he if was standing on the starting line, waiting for the official to fire the gun-

"Hi Denny." Jennifer's sweet, melodious voice seemed to float up out of the phone and into his ear.

"Hello," was all he could muster in response. He took a few steps back up the beach so he could hear better over all the clamor coming from the ocean. "How are you?" he asked, rather timidly.

"I'm okay. You sound far off?"

"Yes. Yes. I'm at the beach. There's a storm coming. Well actually it's not supposed to hit directly here. Way out to sea right now but it's whipping the water up pretty good. But no rain yet. Frederick is its name."

"Oh. Is this why you called me?"

"Yes. That, and Keith almost burned down a building."

"Seriously? I thought I just saw him running on Coal Street the other day."

"Probably so. You know how these things go. You're out on a ten-mile run one day, the next you're committing acts of domestic terrorism."

Jennifer laughed into the phone, then apologized for laughing. God though, Denny missed that sound. Sure, things were good for him here, but he so dearly missed that intimate connection with her. Throughout his life he had come to accept certain tradeoffs as a necessary cost of doing business the way he wanted to, but he couldn't seem to get his heart and mind around this one.

"I'm not sure why I called. I just wanted to hear your voice." He had more to say. Much more to say. Or so he thought. But the words were not ready to come forth.

"I'm glad you called. You know I think of you often and wonder what you are up to."

"Me too." Denny looked again out at the roiling ocean, as it continued to spin and tumble and spit out water and spray and foam. He knew he had to act, had to assume some risks here, and jump back in with both feet. This was sink or swim. "I feel like we made a mistake. Or I made a mistake. I mean you and me. I'm sorry. Maybe I shouldn't have left out like that. Pulling the plug effectively on all of it just like that. I'm sorry. I really am."

The seconds of silence that ensued were about as nerve wracking as Denny had ever gone through, like standing before judge and jury awaiting the verdict to be read. In these moments lives are made, forever altered by conversations and decisions which occur on what may have begun as just another inconsequential day, in the seeming unlimited thread of days, weeks, years. At least he could not be found guilty of withholding his feelings.

"Don't be sorry Denny. Remember, not with me. The first time I saw you again and up through our first date at Angelo's I knew what I was getting into, so it's not like I was some sort of innocent bystander. I could tell when you were here a part of you was somewhere else, and always would be. Like I said that final night at the hotel you would have resented me for pulling you back here again, and from such a great life you've made. Sure, maybe not right away, but eventually. And that would have been awful. For both of us in different ways, to have lived with that."

He let the words sink in. Denny knew she was right, the same as he knew she had been right a few months ago. "I guess I was searching for a little miracle tonight. You know I'm a dreamer."

"I know you are and it's one of the biggest reasons that I care about you like I do."

"Have you been painting much?"

"Yes. And there are a few pieces I put aside to eventually send down to you. My guess is you don't have an interior decorator in North Carolina." The two of them talked a little more. Denny asked about her boys and how their football seasons were going and they talked a little about his running and the cross-country team. And then that was that, they said good night. Denny slowly walked off the beach, and as he did he kicked up a little sand and said aloud, "you were right again Thomas Wolfe."

Early the following morning Denny headed back on foot into the Carolina Beach State Park; his pace was frisky from the get go as he wanted to burn off some of yesterday's events. Though in a way he was glad that there was more of a sense of finality or closure in his mind to this thing with Jennifer, not that it didn't smart some. But it was better than wracking himself with a never-ending series of what-ifs and having a perpetual stream of second guesses coursing through his heart.

Then of course there was this whole matter with Keith, and while he was glad his friend was alright and being taken care of, it did throw the whole plan to meet up and run Richmond together sort of up in the air, which was a big part of why Denny so looked forward to the upcoming race weekend. He hated to ask someone else to go and was doubtful that this close to the actual race he could find another runner to go run it, unless they had been training for something real long themselves. Which if such was the case, they were likely registered somewhere else. These were his thoughts as Denny entered the trails and made his way into the woods, under threatening skies, ominously hinting at the impending heavy rainfall forecast to come ashore.

Which wouldn't necessarily dampen his spirit, since it was quite warm out and incredibly humid, typical of atmospheric conditions ahead of a tropical storm. And such weather was apropos for his current mood; let it rain Denny thought, after checking the radar on his phone before he left out. The outer feeder bands would likely be over top the island well within the hour and hit somewhere within his eight-mile aerobic run. Even though the category two hurricane was predicted to stay well out to sea, the region was expected to see vigorous bouts of heavier rains and wind, as well as some storm surge, and beach erosion. Denny loved the intense energy in the air before and during storms, in the same way that he dug wintery weather and snow. They made him feel more alive and alert when out running, and in harmony with his surroundings.

As Denny knifed through the park at a pace somewhere in the low to mid seven minutes per mile range, his feet barely touching the soft dirt and sand trails, the grayish, white puffy sky overhead began to slowly descend downward, until it almost appeared to be dexterously balancing itself on top of all of the trees. Which had the effect of creating visually, a bright white light in the park, almost eerie looking to Denny as he headed towards Sugarloaf Hill. He heard a low rumbling, moaning noise, that gradually became louder and louder, and seemed to be drawing ever so close to where he ran. The trees right around him began to swirl around, and the wind now angrily whistled towards him; a few moments later he could feel this gargantuan invisible thing on him, like a moist sponge slapping up against his body.

The sky had rapidly turned increasingly darker shades of grey; Denny could actually see the shield of rain advancing through the woods like an unstoppable army marching into battle. He knew it was only a matter of seconds until the rolling bank of fog and moisture would over-take him; there was no chance of out running it even if one would have been so inclined to try. And then it was all on top of him; at first a few big drops of rain, but then it overspread him with sheets of falling rain, nearly blinding him to everything around. Denny was soaked almost before he was cognizant of water being on his body, as he crested Sugarloaf Hill, and looked out towards the Cape Fear River below, which had become eviscerated by clouds and bands of rain, dropping the visibility to only a few hundred feet. It was all so wildly lyrical as he stood there briefly, getting drenched, while marveling at the spectacular splendor of mother nature. Denny turned and headed back down the hill; his shoes now sopped and squished through the mud and wet sand. It all made him want to howl out loud like a wild animal.

And just like that it was over. The rains and wind suddenly ceased, the clouds even parted some, allowing the sun to partially poke some angled rays through. What crazy weather Denny thought, as he continued to hammer out the miles on the trails. Later as he exited the park and got back out onto the roads, Denny could see purplish, grey clouds, and what had to be another feeder band approaching from off the ocean, less than a mile away. He decided to turn it into a challenge and see if he could make it back home before this next one hit. He lost, by one block, but loved every minute of it. Yesterday's troubles seemed to be a distant memory, as he peeled off his soaking wet clothes and took a drink of water from a refrigerated bottle. Another day, another run; the hands of time moved on.

A few days later Keith called; he was back out of the hospital and sounded lucid and sane. "I want to do this more than ever," he said. "I saw everything about to crash down. Like it was happening in slow motion. You know what I mean?"

"Yes. I believe I do. It's like you can step back out of yourself and see the destruction being wrought yet are incapable of stopping it. You sit there and just sort of watch, with an almost morbid sense of fascination. I used to picture what my room would look like through the eyes of the emergency personnel after they had discovered my dead body." Denny paused for a second or two. "Good times, right?"

"Yeah, sounds like it," Keith said. "Anyhow I'm going to finish this fucker even if I have to crawl across the finish line."

The two of them talked some more, predominately about Keith's training and what he had missed, and what to do now going forward. Fortunately, he had had only about a week and a half of no real running, so Denny instructed him to take a few days to ease back into it, then to get in a long run of at least two hours. And the following week to jump right back into the plan. "I'll help get you to that finish line. Nothing has changed much. Trust the process."

“Maybe you should coach the Sixers,” Keith said before saying good night.

The following Sunday Denny had a twenty-four miler on the schedule, the longest run of the plan. He liked the fact that what he was doing might be slightly unconventional, as evidenced by some of the conversations continually being had with fellow runners, who questioned some of the lengths and frequencies of the longer runs he was going on. Charlie joked he ought to be up to about a forty miler by now. But like Denny kept emphasizing to Keith, he himself trusted the process, and he trusted how it had worked for Bert, who was meeting him for the final fifteen miles of the morning jaunt.

The morning air was inspirational for a long run; temperatures had fallen overnight into the upper fifties, and there was little wind to speak of. The past two weeks or so, with the exception of the couple of days the hurricane was nearby, had been such a welcome relief to Denny and fellow runners; autumn had officially begun, and the weather had unofficially begun to noticeably cool down. Which paid dividends in the runs and workouts he was doing; Denny had been freed from the daily war waged against the elements, though Bert had told him that physiologically such training would have long term benefits, once the warmer weather did abate. Such declarative statements were always tempered with the advice to be careful when running long or fast in the heat. But knock on wood, it looked like most of all that could be put to bed for now.

Denny knocked out nine miles on the island by looping southward through the farm, then taking the main road to the marina in the state park, before running back to Kate's Pancake House where he met Bert, who was standing in the parking lot. "Damn bro next time pick another spot to meet up at?"

"Sure. Why's that?"

"I'm getting hungry smelling all this food. I almost went in and bought a pound of bacon to go."

"Now you're making me hungry."

"Let's rock. You got nine in already?"

"Sure did hoss."

"The weather is refreshing," Bert added, as they headed up the main road towards the bridge. "I could run all day in this."

And run they did, at a steady clip in the low eight minutes per mile range. Bert told him that if he could finish this run in that kind of pace and do so without feeling like he was straining himself too much, it would be another positive signpost that he was right where he wanted to be heading into Richmond. And Denny had no reason to doubt any of this; his buddy had correctly predicted how many a key run would play out, as well as when and where some of the rough patches would crop up in his training, and some of the specific workouts that he might struggle to complete. Later in the run, as they made the turn off Cathay Road onto River Road, Bert looked at Denny, and said in a measured, even tone, "you feel like an animal, don't you?"

"I do." And he did, as they clipped off the miles on River Road. Bert talked about his upcoming camping and hiking trips with his family in the mountains, and some of the trails they planned on traversing, and different parks they would visit. Denny enjoyed mostly just listening, especially in the latter stages of the run. The sun was now fully visible in the eastern sky, back out over the Atlantic Ocean. Out on the Cape Fear River, several large boats were headed southward; Denny wondered where they might all be headed to. A bunch of cyclists zipped by them on the road, riding in packs of threes, and fours or more.

Twenty miles into the run Denny was feeling fatigued, though overall, he was alright. He was looking forward to getting out of the bright sun, even though the temperature hadn't warmed up all that much. He had taken water several times, but as per before, he hadn't ingested any food or calories. About halfway into the run he had felt almost insatiably hungry, but the feeling had passed, as he knew from past runs that it would. Plus, he knew that any kind of long run of this magnitude was going to affect him physically, in his legs of course, but also in the shoulders and neck. Mentally too there were effects, mainly just from the sheer amount of time it took to complete such a run, which they did, even dropping the pace into the seven fifties, three of the last four miles.

"Halleluiah," Denny exclaimed, after he hit stop on his watch. "Twenty-four f'n miles."

"Man, you are ready to rock and roll. The hay is almost ready to be placed inside the barn."

"Thanks for the company. And thanks for everything. Twenty-seven days and counting." It was the first time he had said out loud the number of days left. The marathon's website had a running countdown on it, down to the seconds.

"Finish the deal," Bert reminded him. "And let's go eat."

"Will do. I'm buying."

In a somewhat cruel twist of fate, Denny found himself struggling more and more the next week to get out the door; perhaps it was a touch of post long run fatigue from Sunday, or just an adverse by-product of the overall scope of the training already put in, in particular the last two months or so. He would open the book up to the plan, which was bookmarked, hoping to find a small measure of reprieve in the upcoming labor, as if by black magic the contents housed within each daily box were going to rearrange themselves to become less daunting or demanding, though he knew full well what lie ahead. This puzzled and worried Denny, though at this juncture he dared not tell anyone for fear that by doing so, he'd perhaps be giving credence to the weakness he felt, or to the nagging doubts which had suddenly crept in and seemed to be saying "you're all talk and no action." Pride can be a curious and diabolically funny thing; Denny recalled a wise, elderly lady

Mary Jane who was fond of quoting a line from the Bible, "pride goeth before the fall."

Plus, there was a history he had of not finishing things; jobs, projects, relationships, you name it. He had a habit of walking away when things got too tough, or weren't going as planned, or required more work than he had initially anticipated. The list was too long, and too depressing to rehash all of it in his mind, though he reminded himself that much of that was long ago in the past, when his life was ruled by self-deception, and a thousand different fears. He was a much different person today; so each day he took the bit in his teeth, and went out and attacked the run, reminding himself constantly to take it one day at a time, one run at a time, and sometimes, one mile at a time. Trust the process. Don't give in. Not now. Finish the dam deal. He did, however, mention some of this to Bert after much of it had run its course and passed; his friend merely laughed and shrugged it off, saying, "yeah it's a haul for sure."

Denny, like his partner up north Keith, was determined more than ever to complete that which he had set forth to do, though the original vision quest idea had been sort of swept up into the whole marathon project, and the pursuit of the Boston goal. But he figured once again he was right where he was supposed to be, which included glimpses of insight into the longer view of things, and intuitions into the interconnectedness of not only the sentient life around him, but the expansive world of the unseen, that at times seemed as every bit alive as well. He still struggled to translate most any of this, and told Celine that he wished he could carry a dictating machine strapped to his head when he ran, that would also have the ability to decode any relevant thoughts as they popped into his whirring brain, if she knew what he meant?

"No. I don't know what you mean," she tersely replied. "Do the work. You always say trust the process, right?"

"It's refreshing to be quoted I guess."

"Your god dam right it is," she said. Denny knew she spoke form her own experience, and that there weren't going to be shortcuts in any of this.

Chapter 13

It was almost time for the annual Southeastern North Carolina XC Championship races, a local competition held between several clubs and school teams at Hugh McRae Park in Wilmington. Denny and the other Flyers coaches felt like they had a good chance to win two of the coveted team trophies, as their middle school boys and elementary girls teams were looking strong, with good, quality depth on each squad.

"I got the entry sheets last night. There are eleven teams entered on the boy's side for middle school. But I only think we need to worry about two or three of them," Denny told Jim at practice, two days before the meet.

"Cape Fear Academy for sure. Though if we get our three through five to split up their top five we'll be fine." Jim had grown up running scholastically like Denny had, though he was about ten years older. His daughter had graduated last year from one of the local high schools, after having a stellar career capped by a fifth-place finish at states in the 3200-meter run and was currently running collegiately at East Carolina University. The two coaches could talk for hours about training plans, workouts, race strategies.

"Assuming Otto and Zeke go one two."

"I can't imagine they won't. The top times I have seen run are in the low nineteens."

"And they'll be well down into the eighteens. Hopefully," Denny added, with a bit of a nervous chuckle. Like many coaches, he was always hedging his bets, though never in front of any of the kids.

"They are ready," Jim replied, with an assurance that reinforced Denny's positive feelings going into the event.

"The wolf pack is ready to howl as well. Our girls should be a shoe-in. I'm cautiously optimistic about the young boys as well."

"Me too."

The next evening Denny pounded out three times one mile at five-kilometer pace, with three-minute recovery jogs between repetitions. It was tough, relentless running, but he hit his paces spot on, without even looking at his watch at all during the mile repeats. It was the last interval session of the plan; he was now a mere ten days away from the big race, and effectively inside that last block of training time known as the taper. The word taper wasn't actually used in the book, or if it was, it wasn't emphasized. Denny preferred the word sharpening; he felt it carried a more proactive psychological connotation, and he was fond of using the term with his harriers as well. For as he said to Shane once, no-one tapers a spear, do they?

Keith had been religiously texting Denny each day after his runs, as he had been instructed to do after his unfortunate interruption. He had gotten in three long runs, the last of which was twenty miles, and had been averaging over forty miles per week, by far the most mileage he had even run in his modest career. Keith added again, that he just wanted to cross that finish line, even if someone had to catch him when he fell. Denny replied that there would be plenty of race officials and volunteers there to do so, but to make sure they draped a medal around his neck first, as it would make for a better race finish photograph if he did go down.

Denny left work early and arrived at Hugh McRae Park a little before 3:30. The first race, the girls elementary was slated to begin at 4:30. He walked over to the registration table and chatted with a guy and gal that he knew form the race management company that was timing the event and picked up a large manila envelope that contained all of the Cape Fear Flyer's kids race bibs, a plastic sandwich baggie full of safety pins, and a map of the courses in the park. There was always something a touch enchanted about picking up a race packet, whether it be for himself, or for in this case, the forty plus young runners who would be competing today on the grass and dirt terrain. Denny sat down on top of a picnic table beneath one of the large shelters and carefully went through the roster sheet and bibs to make sure nothing was missing. Stacey sat down by him, she was the head of the Club's Sprit Squad, and mother to one of the faster elementary boys on the team. "How's Matty, he excited and ready to run?"

"Oh goodness gracious. I could barely get him to bed last night."

"Right on."

Denny took a pen out of his backpack and started to cross off names as he handed out bibs to some of the runners and parents who began trickling in. He had learned that one can never be too meticulous in such pre-race activities; him and all the coaches who were there would never forget the infamous incident two years ago at a huge invitational track and field meet in Durham, when no-one could locate the bibs an hour before the second day's events, and the ensuing panic as they all frantically scrambled to find the ones needed for the first heats of the 3,000 meters, which seven kids were scheduled to compete in. Finally, they were found on top of a dresser in one of the coaches' hotel rooms, which required Denny and Shane to drive about ninety miles per hour to the stadium, then hand the bibs out the car window to another coach right inside the gates to the stadium, ten minutes before the gun was to go off. "I don't even think we stopped the car," Shane had joked about it later.

Andrea and fellow coach Kensley took care of warming up the young and talented Flyer's girls elementary team, and right from the start they went out strong and formed a pack at the front. Just like their nickname the wolf pack, given to them by Shane last year, since they liked to "hunt medals together." And for the most part they stayed in the front of the field through the finish of the two-mile race; without having to perform any mathematical calculations, the coaches knew their girls had captured the team title, picking up six of the top ten places.

Next the elementary boys got under way, and the younger male counterparts did not disappoint either; Izzy won the race outright, his long black hair flapping around, which had affectionately earned him the nickname "Pre." Like Pre, he was fond of front running, and had the natural ability to do so. Andrea's son Satchell came in second overall, and Matthew eighth, amidst a hodgepodge of other teams' runners, leaving the overall team title to await formal tabulations. "It's going to be close," Jim said to Denny, as they watched the rest of the runners stream into the long chute before the finish line.

While the middle school girl's race began, Denny and Jim took the older boys through the back part of the course; the same course used for high school cross country races locally. Over the past few practices, they had been talking to them about what to do in the race, as a team and as individuals, and about what to possibly expect once the gun went off; though it was always a bit of a fool's errand to handicap things too much at this age. Jim was more precise and technical in conversations, especially on race days, whereas Denny tended to be a little generalized, focused more on easing any tensions the runners might have, trying to get them to relax as much as was possible. It was a good combination, or at least Denny thought so.

Once the middle school girl’s race was nearing its conclusion, the two coaches put their runners through a set of shorter striders on a grassy area back behind the starting corral, then gathered the young men in a tight circle a few minutes before they would line up. Most of the other teams were close by in their various colored singlets, going through their own routines and rituals, trying to shake out the nerves, and ready themselves for the forthcoming showdown. The Flyer's runners may not have known their competitors' names, but they sure as heck knew what colored jerseys their likely closest adversaries were wearing.

"Remember guys I'll be at the mile mark with your splits. Try and stay on the paces we discussed," counseled Jim, as the runners' eyes darted back and forth on him, each other, and all the runners gathered around.

Denny asked them to put one hand in the center of the circle, and as all the hands came together he said, "we are proud of you all for continuing to work hard. This is but another step in the journey. Today we get to have some fun and see what we are made of." The collective jitters of the group were quite evident; the official in charge of the start had summoned the teams to their respective boxes. "And one more thing," Denny said, as the volume of his voice raised, "Don't puke on your shoes. One, Two, Three, FLYERS!"

The team walked over to their assigned box, marked off by numbers made with white spray on top of the grass. "Show time," Denny said, as he winked at Jim, who briefly smiled before taking off to the back side of the park where the one-mile mark would be. And then a few moments later the runners were off, in the typical jailbreak like way which characterized the start of probably ever cross-country race Denny had ever seen, or run in. They had cautioned their proteges not to go out too fast and get swept away in the adrenaline, but both coaches knew that was about damn near impossible to do.

Quickly the amoeba like mass of runners started to disappear from Denny's view as they all headed into another section of the tree filled park. He realized again how much he loved these kids, and just what a blessing it was to play his miniscule role in keeping his beloved sport alive and thriving into the subsequent generations of disciples. Sure, it could be difficult at times; Denny had learned early on there was much more work to it then the Xs and Os. He tried to get to know the kids as much as possible, their personality quirks, how to try and motivate, or to counsel and console. Something he had read many years ago, though where he could not recall, was to always remember that you are coaching people, not runners.

A lot of it too was logistics, and communication; not only with the runners, but with the other coaches, and of course all the parents. And when the races were taking place like now, Denny almost wished he could take a little of the pain for each and every one of the kids or be able to give them a little something extra inside to help them make it on home safe and sound. But he knew that would detract from their experiences; to a person, they all had to learn for themselves firsthand the demands of running, and the rewards which follow.

Denny hadn't rested his older boys up much for this race, with the exception of one lighter practice yesterday. He was pretty confident they could run through it and succeed and stay on track to peak at the State Championship meet in a little less than a month from now. There was always a balancing act training for an 'A' race, and still being able to perform close to the maximum in any subsequent 'B' races. He knew this too from his own personal training, as he stood there and anxiously waited for the first runners to reappear, as they would be coming back through the finish line area at about the half way point of the five-kilometer race.

And then, just as they had hoped, Otto and Zeke emerged from behind the horse stables, running one and two, with a considerable gap between themselves and the next runners. As they passed by Denny said in a conversational tone, "stay cool." He knew he didn't really have to say much of anything to them at that point. About thirty seconds later the chase pack came past him, including Baker who was in fourth place, running so far, the type of race that Denny knew he was capable of, but needed to find the confidence to do. "Stay right there," he enthusiastically hollered to him. They had some chats the past few weeks about trusting his abilities, as he possessed talent on par with the top two runners, but just lacked the long distance running experience. His raw foot speed allowed him to outkick just about anybody; the key was to be in position to utilize such skills.

Ballard and Crispin were in the top ten as well. "Keep digging. Keep digging," Denny called out to them as they passed. Eric and Alberto Juan were not too far behind, amongst the top seventeen or eighteen runners. The team was in excellent position to not only capture the overall title, but to place four, or maybe five runners in the top ten, which would be considered placing and named All-Regional. They are all getting after it he said to himself, as he jogged back over to be further up the final stretch coming into the finish line. Denny saw Jim running back across the park with clipboard in hand, and a stop watch bouncing off his chest. They locked eyes from afar; Denny flashed a thumbs-up signal, which Jim returned with a fist raised in the air.

Otto pulled away late from his teammate Zeke to win. Zeke easily came in second. Baker finished fifth, followed by Crispin in eighth, and Ballard in eleventh, one spot off a podium finish. Once again, mathematics was not required to see that the Flyers had won another team title and had done so in a dominating display. The elementary boys came in a close second in the team chase, and the middle school girls all competed well, but didn't quite possess the ability to stick with the better teams. Denny was thrilled and happy for all of them, as he listened to all the jubilant commentary under the shelter, in the pleasant autumn twilight. "You guys earned this," he said to the gathered kids and parents. "We are thrilled for each and every one of you who came out today and competed with all your heart. Now go home and rest up. Then you can all brag to your classmates in school tomorrow."

"But do your homework first," Andrea called out with a wide grin on her face. And there were many more laughs to he shared as everyone slowly filed back to their vehicles, for the short drives home. On his own drive home, Denny allowed the events of the afternoon and evening to sink in; he was filled with such gratitude and joy that it was almost for the moment overwhelming. His eyes welled up as he crossed over Snow's Cut Bridge, and back onto the island, her lights all twinkling in the night time sky.

That weekend there was one final long run left to be done, though by now the distance of thirteen miles didn't seem too long at all, as such definitions had dramatically shifted the past seventeen weeks. Denny was a week out from the marathon itself. Three hours and ten minutes, over the duration of the past seventeen weeks, had become a part of his persona; the numbers lived and breathed inside of him like only such numbers can for distance runners. Most of his running friends knew them by rote as well; it was how things worked when one was a part of this eclectic, far reaching crowd. They all assured him he was going to do it, and on occasion Denny granted liberties to his mind, which wanted to envision a picture of a race clock with red numbers like 3:08, 3:09, and some seconds, as he approached the finish line.

Boston had grown from a tiny mustard seed back in June, into the ultimate destination he sought; the site of the holy grail of the marathon world. Runners chased after it all over the country, all over the world for that matter, year after year. To be able to see those two letters, BQ, beside his name-Denny knew he could do it, he was certainly ready. Keith called a few days later, he was apprehensive, but ready as well. The clock on the race's website continued to tick down; it was almost time for the curtains to part.

Chapter 14

Keith and Denny met each other Friday evening at the Richmond Convention Center, site of the race weekend's expo. There was an eight-kilometer race, and a half marathon, in addition to the full marathon being held Saturday morning. Keith joked that he was going to inquire if they would allow him to transfer his bib to one of the shorter distances.

"You can always ask," Denny replied, as the two of them made their way towards the appropriate booths to pick up their respective race packets. Denny chatted with a very fit, attractive young volunteer tasked with distributing bibs to those runners who would be starting in the first corral of the marathon, which was based on a predicted finishing time under three hours and thirty minutes. "Good luck," she said, as he walked off to find Keith again.

They wandered around the large expo with many hundreds of fellow runners. Denny found a table with gloves and beanies for sale and purchased two pair of thinner white gloves with '26.2' printed in black on the back sides. He gave one of the pairs to Keith and said, "to your health." Denny had been diligently studying the weather forecast, probably a little too much, based on some friends' comments the past few days. It was going to be a chilly start to the marathon, with temperatures expected at 7:30am to be in the upper thirties, with some wind as well, which was the aspect that Denny fretted the most about. Though sunny skies were called for, with no chance of any rain.

"The wind is supposed to be out of the north predominately," Denny told Keith, while they looked at a large blown up map of the marathon course setting on an easel. "So, it will likely affect us head on most of the first few miles, and then later from miles fourteen through seventeen," he added, as he traced part of the route with his right index finger. "Though we'll have a cross wind in a lot of places too."

"You should have brought a pointer. Or one of those laser type things they use on tv," Keith responded.

"The big bridge could be a little rough," chimed in a guy who was standing behind them. "It's completely exposed going through mile fifteen into sixteen." He showed them on the map.

"Yes. I've read about that," Denny said. "Have you run this before?"

"Be my fifth consecutive year."

"Nice. I'm Denny. And this is Keith. Our first here."

"My first marathon ever," Keith said.

"Cool. You'll love it. Well once you get past the whole running for twenty-six miles part. Oh, I'm Dana. Carl's wife."

"And you must be Carl," Denny said, as he shook his hand.

"Great crowd support out there. Never a dull moment," Carl said.

"I just want to finish. Denny here is going to try and win."

"He's kidding," Denny said, as he picked his new friends' brains for a few more moments before they all parted ways, to the mutual salutations of good luck. And what Carl had told him jived with the information in the course video that Denny had watched multiple times on the marathon's website. There were a lot of rolling, smaller hills on the course, nothing too major, but collectively they could take a bit of a toll. Fortunately, the last few miles were almost completely flat, though Dana did caution to watch out for the last hill before the baseball stadium, at about mile twenty.

Next stop was Denny's sister's and husband's house, located well outside the city to the south and west. Lilly and Ted had cooked up a big pasta dinner for the two runners, which was much appreciated. After a brief tour of the house, which included a high cathedral like ceiling in the front living room, Denny joked that it was nice to see her moving up in the world.

"This coming from someone who lived in an empty apartment for four months?"

"I'll have you know there's a brand-new refrigerator and stove in there," said Keith.

"Yes, there is. He took care of me. And allowed me to indulge in my bohemian fantasies."

"Make yourselves at home here," said Ted. "If the cat bothers you throw her ass outside."

"Hey," protested Lilly, "I've had Annabel for longer than I've known you."

"It's the strangest animal you quite possibly have ever seen. Psychologically scarred beyond repair."

"We'll get along just fine," Keith said.

The two runners were both shown to their own separate bedrooms on the first floor, off to the one side of the kitchen. All of them then sat down for dinner in the dining room. And the meal was divine; angel hair pasta with marinara sauce filled with clams, garlic bread, and a large tossed salad made with vegetables that had been grown in a backyard garden and stored in the root cellar. Both runners were very thankful for the hospitality and pre-race meal, and after hanging out in the living room following dinner, they each decided to turn in early, though Denny doubted he'd get that much sleep tonight. They'd have to be out the door tomorrow morning at about 5:30.

After he was settled in his room, Denny carefully laid out the clothes he was going to race in and pinned his bib onto the bottom front of one of his Cape Fear Flyer's coaches' t-shirts. After some deliberation, and another check of the weather on his cell phone, he decided the full ensemble would consist of shorts, t-shirt, beanie, and gloves. He also had a pair of running socks that went up over his ankles, another small measure he could take to retain body warmth, and protect himself from the elements, while wearing as little clothing as possible, thus reducing the weight being carried, and any drag on his body. What may seem like miniscule differences, when multiplied out over the tens of thousands of steps needed to be taken to cover twenty-six miles, does in fact add up, and can make a difference in performance.

Last, and most important were his running shoes; Denny delicately slid a pair of Saucony Kinetta Relays into his backpack and whispered, "be good to me tomorrow." He also put a blueberry Clif Bar, and two salted caramel GUs into one of the pockets of his shorts, then walked out into the kitchen and cut open two of the wheat bagels he had brought and spread peanut butter on the one he would eat in the morning before they left. Then he placed them in two separate sandwich bags and put inside the refrigerator. Lilly had already set up a cup of coffee ready to brew in the Keurig machine; all he had to do was hit one button.

Start time temperature was currently forecast to be thirty-eight degrees, with an eight mile an hour wind from the north, northeast. By about the time he hoped to be finishing, the temperature was predicted to be forty-four degrees, with an eleven mile per hour wind from the north. The wind was the one thing Denny worried about the most, though he kept reminding himself of something he would always tell his kids, to control what you could control, and don't dwell on the rest. Plus, it could be much worse; it was November after all. Denny laid out a pair of track pants and his heavy UNC Wilmington sweatshirt, which he would wear until as close to the start of the race as he could, before placing them inside a drop bag to be retrieved after the finish. He also put an extra t-shirt, pair of socks, and beanie into the actual bag that he would use as the drop bag. Denny looked again at a map of the downtown which he had printed out, making sure that once again he knew exactly where everything was located, including several parking decks closest to the start line. He had read that the downtown would be crowded, and several streets would be closed. There was a soft rapping at the door, and Keith walked in.

"Hey old sport," Denny greeted him.

"I see you are ready. You weren't kidding around."

"Shit. I almost forgot my watch," Denny said as he found it, and took out of a pocket in his backpack. He also took out the charger and plugged it into a wall socket. It was still at ninety-six percent battery life.

"How do you feel?" Keith asked as he sat down on the one chair that was in the room.

"Me? Okay I hope. I'm ready, that's for sure. Just a matter of executing Saturday," Denny responded. Though there was much more to it than that. Many more things could go wrong than could go right in a marathon. But he knew it wasn't healthy to sit there and speculate about all that. "We shall see," he added, with measured temperance. "I hope the running gods are on our side."

"That would be much appreciated," Keith said rather solemnly. "Hard to fathom that this is actually happening."

"I know."

"Seemed so far off. The day of the race that is. I remember when you first told me about all this. We were running the Ukes. Heck you were still living up there. In P A."

"Was a lot warmer too."

"And now it's like damn. This marathon is actually about to occur." Keith pulled his cellphone out from a pants pocket. "In a little under ten hours!"

"It's wild isn't it?"

"I'm not sure wild is the word I would use to describe it," Keith laughed, with a twinge of nervousness.

"Think of tomorrow as a celebration of sorts. A culmination of months of hard work and training." Denny sensed his buddy could use a little propping up, some positive reinforcement. "You've travelled one hell of a road to get to where you are at this very moment. Tomorrow is the icing on the cake. And all of this is just a beginning, the sky is the limit my friend."

"I don't know what to think. Maybe it's best to not think too much more and just do it right?"

"Yes. Let it flow. Use the adrenaline, and energy from all the other runners and the crowd. Like those people at the expo said it'll be crazy out there. It'll get hard at the end. You know I've never sugar coated any of it. The last few miles will be the hardest you've ever done."

"Well knowing I have that to look forward to makes it all worthwhile I guess." This time when he laughed, much of the nervous tension had evaporated.

"Love you my man. And I'll be there at the finish."

"Thanks for everything," Keith said, as the two longtime friends shared a hug. "Don't forget to set your alarm," Keith added as he walked on back out of the room, and pulled the door closed. In all of his own preparations, Denny had lost sight a bit as to what this all meant to Keith, but he was reminded of that when he saw the tears welling up in his friend's eyes. It was much more than just a race for him; it was an affirmation of who he had become.

Before Denny laid down and attempted to get some rest, he pulled out a blue envelope from another compartment in his backpack. It had arrived in the mail a few days ago from Jennifer; he was still hesitant to open it up, since it seemed to him to be the perfect situation to have unread communication from her. Though after holding what felt like a greeting card in his hands for several moments, he did finally open the envelope. On the front of a card was a picture of a big medal hanging from a ribbon draped around a little boy's neck, that all looked like a water color painting done in an art class at school. The inside of the card had scrawled in squiggly letters "You are always a champion in my book." Denny smiled, as he read Jennifer's own personal words of encouragement, and looked at the drawing she had done of the Boston Marathon's iconic unicorn. He placed the card back in the envelope and set it on top of the small table by the bed and turned off the lamp light. There was dead silence throughout the house, save for the tick tick tick tick from a clock hanging on one of the walls in the bedroom. How fitting, Denny thought.

As he laid there awake, so many people floated in and out of his mind; people he had encountered at some point in time through running, stretching all the way back to his earliest days with the

Booster Club Track and Field program in Lehighton, and up through the present to the people he ran with, and the kids he coached. The faces he saw, suspended there for a few brief moments, as if Denny could reach out and lay a palm on their foreheads. Some like Traci Jean had passed on; others had names that escaped him. He could see some of his old coaches too, like Richard Miller walking with a hitch across the infield, and Mr. Bloomfield, with stopwatch in hand calling out splits, or asking his gasping runners to check their pulse rates again after another hard lap. There were so many people; they came and went, or in some cases like Trent, returned back into Denny's little world once again. He felt an irrepressible sense of love, emanating out from an astral plane where they had all shared the sacred bonds of the sport of running. Such a sweet, simple thing. Denny knew in the grand scheme of things it didn't matter all that much how he fared tomorrow, after all it was just one race, one run, one day, in the eternal building blocks of time. Sure, he would try with all his might to cover twenty-six point-two miles in the least amount of time that he could; he would spill his guts out there on the roads, as he tried to do whenever he donned a race bib and toed the line. But that was secondary to the priceless, shared gifts the sport had endowed him and others with. Humility, courage, sacrifice; the list could go on and on, for it was each person's to make.

At some point he did drift off to sleep, though before he knew it he heard the sound of the alarm going off on his phone. The day itself did not require any more hype; Denny knew as he walked into the dark kitchen to make coffee, that any extraneous adrenaline at this hour was counterproductive, there would be more then he could possible ever need available closer to gun time. For now, it was a matter of taking care of one thing, then the next; following the routine he had already laid out. There was light under the door of the room Keith was in; Denny saw as he walked back into his. He checked the weather app on his phone; it was thirty-six degrees in Richmond, with a wind speed of seven miles per hour out of the northeast. Denny drank his coffee and slowly, methodically got dressed.

When Denny came back out of his room, Keith was sitting on the couch in the living room. "Time to earn the rent money," he said.

The marathoners left out of the house; it was pitch black and cold outside. "Once the sun comes up it'll feel warmer," Denny said as he backed out of the driveway.

"How many times have you checked the weather this morning?"

"Remarkably just twice."

On the thirty-minute ride into the downtown, Denny and Keith chatted away about pretty much anything that didn't have to do with the upcoming race; it was a bit strange, but comforting, and each of them understood without verbal acknowledgement, that discussion about how the Eagles maniacally kept losing close games, or how Ron really liked playing on the defensive line this season, was much better for their constitutions, then any running banter. Though when the skyline of Richmond became visible in the pinkish grey dawn, Denny could feel a slight churn in his stomach. Once downtown, police directed them to one of the numerous parking decks being utilized by the thousands of athletes who would be descending upon the area.

After parking, the two of them sat in Denny's Rav4 for several minutes, and sort of let the atmosphere sink in, while remaining warm as well. Runners were milling about in the parking garage, on the streets; the energy was visceral, though Keith seemed to be looking a bit haggard and pale, perhaps being confronted first hand with the upcoming travail. The race's start was still over an hour away.

"Let's start walking up to the start area. We can find some bathrooms, and the drop bags location." Denny guessed they were seven or eight blocks away from the starting line.

"Okay. You're the boss."

Once they got out onto the streets, some of the color seemed to return to Keith's face, and he became a bit more animated again. "I felt like I was going to hurl back in that garage," he said.

"I understand. Best to wait though until after the race."

"I'll try and remember that."

Walking felt good and served to loosen the legs up. Denny didn't plan on doing any kind of a warm up run; the first few miles would serve as such, and most people like Bert agreed that it was best to save all your running capital for the race itself. Bert had texted good luck while they had been sitting in the car, as had several other friends last night and this morning. Denny knew too that a few people would be following his race; Charlie and Xavier had both asked for his bib number so they could track him in real time on a free app provided by the marathon. The sidewalks were now teeming with people. "What a blessing this is," Denny said aloud.

"Talk to me in five hours," Keith replied.

"Buck up sailor."

"I need to take a crap."

About ten minutes before the marathon was about to begin the two friends parted ways. Denny put both his arms on Keith's shoulders and said, "take it a mile at a time. And relax man, it's just a job."

"I'm ready. Let's do this," he replied. "You are going to kill it." Denny could see the fire in Keith's eyes. He himself jumped back out of that corral and made his way forward up the sidewalks. I am going to kill it, he thought, as he climbed over a metal barrier and got inside his starting corral. Denny felt confident, fit, and prepared, though he knew not to get too cocksure, and do something foolish early on like go out too fast. Twenty-six miles is a long way, irrespective of fitness. A local high school band was introduced; they would be performing the national anthem. Denny took off his Eagles beanie and tucked it under his left arm, as he lightly pressed his right hand up against his chest.

After the stirring rendition of The Star-Spangled Banner, Denny took off an old, ratty long sleeve shirt he had been wearing, and tossed it over the metal barriers into a growing pile of miscellaneous clothes, which would later be donated to local homeless shelters. He put his beanie back on, made sure the laces in his shoes were double knotted, and stopped and reset his Garmin watch back to all zeros. The mayor of Richmond was introduced and got on the PA system and bellowed "Are you reaadddy!?"

Thousands of runners, and spectators lining the streets responded unequivocally that they were ready. "On your marks. Set. Go!" the mayor wailed, as the loud shriek of a horn also blared into the morning sky. Denny could see up ahead the sub-elite men in the field take off down the street; one of them would win the race in around two hours and fifteen minutes if history was an accurate guide. Those right around him began to slowly walk forward, then break into a light trot; about ten to fifteen seconds later Denny crossed under the start line stanchion and started his watch, as his race had officially begun. "Relax," he told himself. "Be cool."

The first part of the race proceeded out of the immediate downtown area and onto some wider streets, which allowed the tightly packed mass of marathon runners to find a little room and spread out some. Denny kept checking his watch; he was running at about a 7:30 pace a half of a mile in and had just pulled ahead of the three hour and fifteen-minute pace group, which for psychological purposes he wanted to keep behind him, even this early on. “Don't let them pass me,” he said aloud, which was drowned out by the euphoric racket on, and all around, the course. And like Keith had mentioned last night, it did feel surreal to be actually running the race, after all those months of buildup. Almost before he knew it, Denny had gone through the mile mark in 7:21; perhaps a little too fast, but right about where he wanted to be. Besides he could barely feel a thing, except a bit of a cold breeze on his exposed skin.

The race made its way into some more residential sections of the city, and certain roads the course took were divided by grassy berms with rows of trees. Denny passed numerous people out holding homemade signs and ran by the first of the advertised bands playing live music. "Wow. Tears For Fears. I haven't heard that in twenty-five years," he remarked to a runner beside him.

"Me either," she said.

Denny felt alright and made the decision early on to start hitting mile splits around the goal pace of 7:15, and to do so mostly by feel if possible; he didn't want to be compelled to be constantly checking his watch. He thought about what Bert had said again about expending energy and trying to avoid wasting any. Denny reasoned that every time he did check his watch a small physical, and also mental toll was being paid; so, for the most part he would only check it when at the mile markers, and then make any adjustments if needed. Though he suspected at some juncture in the race, the marathon would be like any other race, in that it would become simply a matter of running as fast as one could until they got to the finish line, with the hope that by then, all available resources will have been depleted. Or to put it another way, Denny couldn't imagine getting to say mile twenty and thinking, okay I should pick my pace up now as I seem to be going too slow. But he knew he was pretty much a novice to the distance, and a good bit of all this would have to be figured out on the fly. Other peoples' advice and knowledge would only take him so far.

The energy of the spectators was infectious; block after block seemed to be full of wildly supportive people out braving the cold to cheer on people who were strangers for the most part. Denny did get a "good job coach," shout out, which amused him. He thought about the team back home; in two weeks they'd all be going to the State XC meet at Hagan Stone Park, which was in the central foothills of North Carolina. Last year it was freezing cold and quite windy, which put today's weather in perspective. Denny went past the four-mile sign in 7:12. Just up ahead it looked like the course was crossing a major boulevard, as policemen were in the road, and a large group of people were standing near the corner, in front of what looked to be like a big restaurant, and a drug store. As Denny ran by absentmindedly glancing about, he saw a man standing on the edge of the crowd who reminded him of his Dad. He had on a red beanie and grey hooded sweatshirt and was wearing a pair of those big aviator like sunglasses. God it's way too soon to hallucinate, Denny told himself.

There were some rolling hills on the course as advertised, as the field journeyed westward into suburban Richmond. Denny grabbed some HEED at an aid station just below a bigger hill, that went for a little over two blocks, before cresting, and then sloping back downward. He tried to not slow his pace down while running up them, and to allow gravity to assist on the descents, and to attack the hills one at a time. At the top of another hill right beyond the six-mile marker, a lady standing in a front yard informed him and the small pack of runners around him, that a nice downhill stretch was awaiting them beyond the upcoming right-hand turn. "I hope she's right," one of the runners responded.

"I live right by the beach we have almost no hills," Denny said to her, but she did not respond. But the friendly spectator was indeed correct; the course began going down a long decline at a healthy angle, headed towards what looked like the entrance to a shopping center, tucked into the hollow about a half mile or more away. Denny aired it out a bit; by now the field of runners had become fairly strung out, so for the most part a runner could run the line they chose to take, without having to maneuver much around others.

Just then he ran over the timing mat at the ten-kilometer mark; the clock read 44:52, and as Denny started to do some calculations, he remembered that the time was actually the gun time, and not his chip time. Which meant he could subtract about twenty seconds, or maybe a little more off of it. Denny wondered if his friends tracking him back in North Carolina had just gotten a text with his time. Puts a little pressure on me though now doesn't it, he conversed with himself; but after he had gotten the math all worked out he realized he was off to a solid start. A little voice inside kept saying very softy, but with an unmistakable air of conviction, "go for it. Fucking kill this thing. You are in shape to do so." Denny was determined more than ever now to push his stack of chips into the center of the table, and to go for broke.

The next few miles went by rather smooth; soon Denny was descending into a shallow valley in which the James River ran through the bottom of. The long bridge spanning part of the valley was high up, and afforded a spectacular view of the river, which had bigger rocks all scattered about and sticking up above the surface. It reminded Denny of crossing the Weissport Bridge and looking down at the Lehigh River, all those times he ran across it when up in

Pennsylvania. That all seemed so far off; but as he neared the end of the bridge he thought about Jennifer. Much of the red-hot intensity had cooled, and for a while Denny sort of went emotionless. Plus, the sadness wrapped into it all could be a bit debilitating too. But time itself has a remarkable way of mending our bruises; today Denny felt nothing but tender affection from afar. "Take care, be well," he whispered into the wind, right before he exited off the bridge, and ran by the ten-mile sign.

His watch read 7:09, and the elapsed time was now 1:12:06, which put him ahead of pace. But Denny cautioned himself, knowing that being too fast early could be a recipe for disaster later; he had followed the plight of too many a marathon run by friends and colleagues of his in the Wilmington Road Runners who had gone out aggressively quick, only to crash and burn later. And most of them were very experienced, talented runners. A couple of minutes here or there could be the difference in success or failure; for now, Denny told himself to just keep it rolling, as he ran along River Road, which would pretty much parallel the James River for the next couple miles, as the course wound its way through some charming countryside. Just like so many of his training runs back home; heck the roads even shared the same name. Denny shook his arms and rubbed his shoulders as he continued eastward, into the second third of the marathon. Over here, there were much less people out watching, and if it weren't for the presence of other runners, it would be very possible to forget one was actually participating in a race. But all of that mattered little to Denny; his solitary objective was to continue to click off the miles.

After cresting a short hill and passing the thirteen-mile sign, Denny could see an electronic clock and timing mat up ahead. It was a welcome sight he had been looking forward to since going through the tenth mile; as he came down the hill, the numbers read 1:32:56. A high-pitched pinging noise recorded the time; once again Denny subtracted off twenty-seconds and rounded it to

1:32:30; a little too fast, though on the flipside, this gave him a bit of a buffer time wise. 1:37:30 is what he needed to run the next half marathon in, and at the moment he felt like that was certainly doable. Keep rolling, keep covering ground he told himself again. He knew in the back of his mind that there was still a hell of a lot of work left to be done, and that in reality, this thing was perhaps just getting started.

The course headed back into another commercial district, in a suburb south of the downtown, quite the visual contrast from the previous few miles. Denny ran by another band out playing, but he didn't recognize the song. The sun was now fully visible, rising slowly up through the eastern sky, and for the first time in the race he felt a tad bit warm. But as he took a left turn and headed towards the big bridge at mile fifteen, Denny was reacquainted with that pesky head wind out of the north. He told himself not to panic, nor to make any adjustments. And although it was not planned, and could yet still prove to be a fatal error, he did have a small cushion of time built in. Math and meteorology were on the brain, as Denny caught his first glimpse of the big bridge looming ahead.

There's an old adage in sports, that sometimes it’s better to be lucky than to be good. And perhaps as another signpost as to how the whole thing would ultimately play out, that is all the months of training followed by the actual race itself, just as Denny was about to commence crossing the mile long, completely exposed bridge, he came up on a guy who had to be about six feet four inches tall, and well over two hundred pounds. Duck in and ride him across the bridge thought Denny, which is exactly what he did, as did two other runners to boot. Despite this fortuitous break, Denny still had to mash his teeth and power through the wind, as the Richmond skyline glistened all silvery and pristine in the morning sunlight, when he did shoot an occasional look up ahead.

Denny wondered how Keith was doing and did some loose calculations as to where exactly he might be on the course. The elapsed time was a little over 1:51; if Keith was maintaining a ten minute per mile pace, he would be somewhere around mile eleven, perhaps now enjoying the views of the James River as he ran on River Road. Or maybe he was still up on that high bridge, looking down at the river like Denny had done before. I wonder if it would remind him of the Lehigh too, Denny pondered.

Some general fatigue had crept into Denny's legs, and his upper torso too, specifically around the shoulder blades. At the next aid station, he took a cup of water, and slowed enough to drink most of it, something he was loathe to do. He hadn't taken any calories in from the food in his pockets, something he realized he should have done sooner. But at this point in the race, with less than ten miles left, he didn't want to take the chance of developing any sort of gastrointestinal issues; on top of that, he was not hungry whatsoever. No, he would run on the fuel he had inside of him, not having the experience to know what a crucial mistake that could be.

Ironically the route then took him, and a couple of the runners who had happened to form up into a little pack the previous half mile or so, past what had to be an Italian restaurant, since the distinct, and mouthwatering aroma of pizza wafted out over onto the street. "Dam that smells good," Denny said to this younger runner who was right aside of him and had asked him a bit ago what pace they were running on his watch.

"You aint kidding," he replied.

Just then Denny saw that same shorter guy in the grey sweatshirt and red beanie; he kind of locked in on him from up the road say forty, fifty meters away, and noticed that this man seemed to be doing the same thing to him as well. Though with thousands of runners, and thousands of spectators, this wasn't all that unusual per se; however, as Denny got closer, a peculiar, mysterious sensation enraptured his body, as this man starting clapping his hands, waving and hollering, while remaining fixed on him visually, at least as much as could be discerned through dark glasses. As Denny got within twenty meters, fifteen, ten-his whole body seemed to instantly leap out of him, and everything on the periphery blurred out, except the man in the center of the image, who became clearer and clearer...

Oh my gosh it's him; the words stunned Denny as he heard himself utter them in a flash inside his head. The feeling in his body returned straightaway as well; the optics resumed their normal physical properties. It was his father, standing there, cheering him on like mad; he called out, "go Denny" as he went by, and added, "looking good," which Denny clearly heard as he continued to run, unsure for a few brief moments if he should have stopped, or said something in return? He was at an absolute loss to comprehend any of this, but that quickly he was in the next block, and then in the next one after that.

He could put together the how's of it; certainly, his sister must have arranged all of this, but the why's? That was the sixty-four-thousand-dollar question. Was something wrong, was he sick? Or dying? He looked fine standing back there, but that might not necessarily mean anything. Denny raced on and let it all percolate; before he knew it, he had passed the seventeen-mile mark. One down, nine to go he said to himself, as he had begun counting down the last ten miles. He wondered again about his Dad, it just didn't make any sense. Would he be there at the finish? Denny didn't know. Denny didn't know anything. Therefore, he ran, going through mile eighteen in 7:03. Focus, concentrate he told himself. We've got a job to do.

The big twenty-mile mark lie ahead, which not only served as the next official timed checkpoint, but represented the gateway to the abyss, the point beyond which the human body is not designed to be able to properly function, and retreats into a desperate survival mode. In race terms, the last ten kilometers is where the marathon can be won or lost. Victories, PRs, BQs, are made here, or tragically lost. It's the final leg where heroes are born, dreams attained; where months of hard work starts to pay dividends, as exhausted runners encounter thresholds they never thought they had the stamina, and fortitude to surmount. But it can be a harsh sport; as for some runners, this is where everything they've worked so hard for, crumbles to pieces.

Denny recalled again the conversation at the expo, and the warning about the devilish little hill before the twenty-mile mark, at the minor league baseball stadium, visible way up ahead. When his watch beeped at mile nineteen, Denny didn't look; he wanted to be surprised by the clock at mile twenty. Besides, he was definitely into the part of the race where pace had become a bit immaterial; the strategy now was simple, keep moving forward, and get to the finish line in one piece.

And he had begun his prayer ritual, something that he had done on his longer training runs. Right after he passed a mile marker, Denny would recite the Lord's Prayer, saying each line slowly in his head. Once completed, he would recite the Serenity Prayer, again slowly, line by line. After that, he would count from one to ten, then back down to one. Usually once this was all finished, Denny would have covered three to four tenths of a mile, which would leave say six tenths or so of a mile left to be run, before the process would begin anew.

While he said the prayers, the trick was to think of nothing else, to focus on the words and phrases themselves, and the meanings inherent within. He looked up and saw the stadium in full view just off to the right, and then took the small, steep hill rather strong, though it did take a toll on his legs, which by now were fairly sore, and felt like they had a fair amount of lead inside them. Denny thought about Keith again, and tried to think of where he might be again in the race, but it all got too muddled up in his brain so he gave up, and simply added go Keith in his head. Denny wondered if he knew about his Dad coming, or if he had any hand in it.

A clock was now visible on the side of the road. He wished that Bert could see what he was seeing, or how it would be nice if this was just another of their long runs together. Though the truth of it was, there was no other place Denny would rather be; it was the deal he had signed on to, and he was so very grateful for the challenge of it all. Like countless other runners have heard a billion times over, if it were easy, everyone would be doing it. Denny hit twenty miles in 2:21:16.

The course made its way into another residential area, and Denny once again thought about his father. Perhaps all the years had helped to melt away the animosity between the two of them. He knew he could be real stubborn, after all he had inherited that from his dad. Maybe it was just time, time for this whole sordid thing to be put behind them. Denny had done so many horrible things; he had been a serial liar, a cheat and a thief, and had abused any semblance of trust that had existed between him and others, like his father. And after all, it was him who callously spewed into the phone that dreadful night, "I never want to talk to you again." Denny had been sick, real sick. He could never possibly realize the total effect his behavior had on those who loved him; but being with Jennifer had also shown that with enough mercy, and good intentions wounds could heal, and new relationships could be forged on top of the ashes of the old. He peeked over at some people gathered on someone's front lawn, half expecting to see his father there. A couple of yards later, Denny passed the twenty-one-mile mark.

Denny felt like his face was falling off, and sensed that he was moving much slower, gauged against the speed at which the scenery went by. He hadn't looked at his mile split at twenty-one, but now wished he had. His left calf was cramping and would periodically send out nasty little shooting pains. And the bottom of his right foot felt real sore and tender. After running past a park that he swore would never end, Denny finally got to the mile twenty-two sign; this time he checked his watch and was pleasantly surprised to see the time of 7:23, as he was worried he had slipped back into the eights. The next mile went by manically slow, and Denny had run it slower, in a time of 7:32; but he took it in a heartbeat as again he felt like he was moving much slower than that.

The course wove its way back into a more commercial, and industrial section of the sprawling city. Reliable signs that the finish couldn't be too far off. But there were still three miles to go, three bloody miles. Denny thought about Keith and wondered how the bloody bastard was doing. And then questioned why his thoughts were coming through with a British accent. He was exhausted, hot, thirsty again, and his legs were about to be overrun by lactic acid, as it now had become somewhat of a struggle to maintain a normal cadence. Denny almost clipped a big orange cone near the center line of the course, just as he was about to pass two policemen. He checked his watch, breaking the rules he had established early in the race. The elapsed distance read 23.57 miles; he could now start counting it down by tenths of a mile. One at a time. Less than a five-kilometer race to go. Denny made a conscious effort to pick up the pace, or perhaps more accurately, he attempted to stop the pace from sliding further backwards.

He pictured Charlie running beside him, trying to keep him on task, and on pace. Denny even started to converse with him, happy to have him out there running in his regular attire of baggy, colorful shorts, with his longer, greying hair flapping in the wind. "You got this man. Keep grinding," Charlie said to him, as they made their way down a street with some taller office buildings on either side.

"Thanks for being here."

"This is much more fun than tracking you on a phone."

Denny did keep grinding, while telling himself that he hadn't done shit yet, that it didn't mean a thing unless he closed the deal and finished it off. It was something he had done in the past, a gimmick employed to avert complacency, and to keep the motivation dialed up at a ten late in a run or race. He knew he was going to BQ, he knew he was going to break 3:10, but he still had to actually do it. Denny wasn't so sure it made sense, but Charlie assured him that it did, before bidding him adieu, and fading off the scene before the twenty-four-mile sign. The time 7:24 preciously illuminated on Denny's watch. Fuck yeah, he yelled inside his head, I'm not finishing this thing slowing down.

Denny started reciting the Lord's Prayer, but this time when he got to the lines, "forgive us our trespasses, as we forgive those who trespass against us," he paused, and his mind stayed suspended on those critical words. He repeated it a few more times, and at some point, he could hear Jennifer's voice now reciting those lines as well, in perfect unison. And suddenly that first night in her basement, and the long walk in the woods past the falls came rushing back at him; he could see it all, the vivid colors in the paintings, all the swirly images of kaleidoscopic layers, the disfigured red face. The pine trees, the sight of the lake below; all of it seemed to be clicking into place as Denny continued to run on. The whole endeavor had become more than just attaining the finish line; it had metamorphized into a journey towards forgiveness, for his father, for himself. The one thing he seemed incapable of doing on his own accord. It was all inseparable; each was conditioned upon the other.

Denny hit twenty-five miles in 7:23; he was back in the heart of the downtown. And the ice that had accumulated around his own heart, continued to melt away onto the asphalt of the marathon course. Once again, he went through his prayer rituals, this time tears welled up in his eyes. The finish line seemed so close that Denny could taste it in his mouth; he was about to crush his goal, and to qualify for the fabled Boston marathon, but all of that had become perhaps a footnote to something much bigger that was occurring for him out on the roads today. All those miles he had run, in Pennsylvania, in North Carolina; every single one of them had to be run in order to get to where he was at that very moment. For if we stay patient, keep moving forward, get up when we fall down, miracles can and will transpire. We find salvation out here, in an infinite amount of ways. Moved by what stirred in him, Denny blurted out, "keep going Keith," which may have startled a fellow competitor close by him. "Almost there," he added, a bit more evenly.

"Yep," the other runner managed to reply.

Denny's legs were shot to hell and must have weighed a hundred pounds each. He tried to lose himself in the cheering crowds that became progressively larger. The atmosphere was indeed electric again, as it had been all those hours ago back at the start, which inspired Denny to inhale as much of it as he could, in the hopes that it would propel him to cover the last few city-blocks as fast he could. He gave thanks to Bert and Mr. Pfzinger for their guidance and expertise; Denny felt confident going in, and had remained confident throughout the marathon, which is the best testament any runner could give about a training plan. The last few miles had been some of the hardest in his life; Denny had taken things to the very edge and danced on the knife blade.

He rounded the final turn onto a wide avenue now lined with people several rows deep, passed by the twenty-six-mile sign, and began the steep descent to the finish line. There was no need to look at his watch now. Instead he fixed his gaze at the finish line stanchion, spread across the street, like an oasis of land in the middle of the stormy sea. Today, he would choose to step ashore.

About a hundred meters from the finish line, an unmistakable voice rose up from the swell of fans; Denny heard, "go Denny. Go son go!" This time his sister was alongside his dad; they both waved their arms hysterically, and when he passed by Denny pointed with his right arm and waved back to them. Then for the first time Denny saw the electronic clock, and the red numbers, that read from left to right 3,0,6... followed by the ticking seconds. Moments later he pumped his fist in the air as he crossed underneath and ran across the painted finish lie. As he slowly, painfully came to a stop, and began the long walk through the finish line chute, Denny was overcome with such raw emotions that he began to cry uncontrollably. What he felt, what he was feeling was beyond anything he could have possibly fathomed. A volunteer draped a medal around his neck, and another handed him a finisher's blanket. I did it, he said to himself. We did it.

Denny bent over once he got through the chute and tried to stretch his legs but it was no use; it was a difficult chore to even walk. He grabbed a bottle of water from atop a table and took a long, much needed drink, then heard his father's voice calling out to him from behind. Denny slowly turned to face the man he had sworn off and had been estranged from for almost ten years; he could see tears in his eyes as well, as father and son embraced in a hug. "I'm so sorry. So very sorry."

"Me too. It's over now."

Sudden cramps in both legs almost dropped Denny to his knees, as the two of them made their way very slowly back to the UPS trucks which had the drop bags, and warm, dry clothes. They chatted about the race, in a way which belied the separation that had been between them. As Denny stopped, to get in line for his bag, his father said, "well I guess congratulations are in order." He smiled and shook his son's hand. "The torch has been passed."

"I'll be honest. I was gunning for it."

"I know."

"How so?"

"Because I would have been doing the same thing. Don't forget, I am a runner too Denny."

With that, they both laughed. A few minutes later Denny began the painful process of changing his clothes. It felt like heaven to take off his shoes and socks, and also to put on a sweatshirt and new beanie. "Let's go see your sister. I'm afraid by now she's thoroughly bored with all of this. I promised her a slice of pizza at the after party."

"Okay. I'm going to go back up and wait for Keith. I'll meet you guys there in a bit."

"That's right. Bring your buddy on home. We have plenty of time to talk."

"Yes, we do Dad." As Denny watched him head off, he called out, "hey, how'd you like to go to Boston?"

Back up past the finish line, Denny found a spot on the grassy hillside to sit and watch the race, but he kept sliding back down it since it was so steep, and he lacked the leg strength to stop it from happening. A young boy found this to be quite amusing; he hoisted himself up the hill and slid down it himself. Denny smiled at him, and figured out a way to stabilize his legs, though that soon proved to be too much work, so he walked down instead to an open spot along the metal railing by the side of the course. Runners were pouring down the hill in droves, in various states of elation, distress, relief; it was all plastered on their weathered faces.

Denny cheered some as he watched, and waited for Keith, and as he did so, he reflected on what he had accomplished out there this morning. He had run one of the best races of his life, in front of two people he had known his whole life. Denny knew this vision quest of his was not over, and probably would never be. Besides which, it was just the name of a movie he vaguely recalled from the eighties. He was reminded of the Matsuo Basho poem, *A Narrow Road to a Far Province*, in which the author writes about those who are perpetually travelling, and how that their destination was no longer home, but that home had become the journey in and of itself. Running, and the runs themselves, had become home for Denny.

The words from the legendary running coach Joe Vigil, "ask nothing from your running, and you'll get more than you ever imagined," touched something deep inside his soul this crisp, sunshine-filled fall morning.

The minutes continued to tick by past the four-hour mark, as Denny alternated between standing, and leaning over onto the barrier, though he was afraid he would tip over a section of railing onto the course. He continued to send prayers out to the running gods to shepherd Keith home, while also thinking about all the junk food he wanted to eat later, like a bag of Swedish fish Andrea had sent with him. And a burger sounded dam good too, or that pizza advertised over at the celebration party. Denny was mulling all this stuff over when he saw Keith coming on down the blessed hill. As he got closer, Denny started yelling to him; Keith finally saw him and broke into one of the biggest grins he had seen all morning. He angled across the road and came over towards Denny, who stuck an arm up in air; they high fived as Keith exclaimed, "I can't freaking believe it," before ambling on down the rest of the hill like he was on a bed of marbles, and then also crossing the finish line.

And that is a big part of the ultimate joy in this whole thing, we get to share it with each other. We share the triumphs, the accomplishments, the goals set, and the goals reached, we share in the pain, the setbacks, and the heartbreaks. We laugh, we cry; we learn, we grow. And wake up the next day to do it all over again.

44834543R00141

Made in the USA
Columbia, SC
20 December 2018